BASICS
ARCHITECTURE
03

Jane Anderson

architectural design

Ethical:
aware-
ness/
reflect-
ion/
debate

ava
academia

An AVA Book

Published by AVA Publishing SA
Rue des Fontenailles 16
Case Postale
1000 Lausanne 6
Switzerland
Tel: +41 786 005 109
Email: enquiries@avabooks.com

Distributed by Thames & Hudson (ex-North America)
181a High Holborn
London WC1V 7QX
United Kingdom
Tel: +44 20 7845 5000
Fax: +44 20 7845 5055
Email: sales@thameshudson.co.uk
www.thamesandhudson.com

Distributed in the USA & Canada by:
Ingram Publisher Services Inc.
1 Ingram Blvd.
La Vergne TN 37086
USA
Tel: +1 866 400 5351
Fax: +1 800 838 1149
Email: customer.service@ingrampublisherservices.com

English Language Support Office
AVA Publishing (UK) Ltd.
Tel: +44 1903 204 455
Email: enquiries@avabooks.com

ISBN 978-2-940411-26-9

10 9 8 7 6 5 4 3 2 1

Design by Jane Harper

Production by AVA Book Production Pte. Ltd., Singapore
Tel: +65 6334 8173
Fax: +65 6259 9830
Email: production@avabooks.com.sg

Project: House Tower
Location: Tokyo, Japan
Architect: Atelier Bow-Wow
Date: 2006

Atelier Bow-Wow describe their
approach as the 'practice of lively
space'. This sectional perspective
drawing was made as part of a study
for the book Graphic Anatomy to
catalogue the houses that they had
designed. Their intention was to
produce drawings with a spatial
depth, which describe the various
relationships between spaces,
components and objects, and which
show the building's context, its
occupants and the evidence of their
occupation.

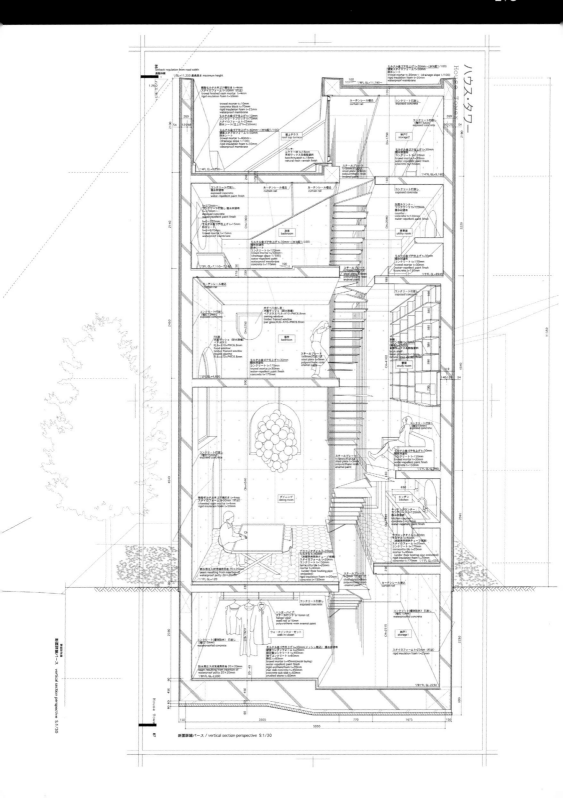

断面詳細パース / vertical section perspective S:1/30

Contents

Architectural design

The architectural design process is as diverse as the people who practise it. The variety and richness of approaches to the subject can be seen in the radical differences between architects' work. In any architectural competition, no two entries will be the same. What inspired the architect? Why is there no one 'correct' answer to a given architectural problem? Talk to any architect or study their work and you will begin to notice that there is both method and inspiration behind their approach. This book sets out to explain the process of design by tying together the experiences of those involved in the practice and learning of architecture.

Architectural projects are generally discussed by the public and the profession after they have been built and handed over to the client. At this point a degree of hindsight and post-rationalisation makes the complicated story of a project's development intelligible. However, the process of architectural design itself is still shrouded in mystery, little discussed and rarely represented in publications or interviews with architects. What value do we place on the wastepaper basket of crumpled preliminary sketches or rough concept models?

The way that an architect designs – the process that they follow – is constructed by the individual; it is entirely built around their own values, skills and preoccupations. It is important that architects are conscious of, and reflect upon, their own design process; not only because this is what they bring to a design project as creative individuals, but also to enable them to take ownership of the process in order to avoid carelessly repeating outdated or obsolete actions.

previous page:
Project: Villa Mairea
Location: Noormakku, Finland
Architect: Alvar Aalto
Date: 1939

Initial sketch design for a hilltop house showing the relationship between the plan, section, site and details. Aalto designs by considering both large- and small-scale elements; landscape and architecture; fragments and the whole picture.

Alvar Aalto Museum, drawings collection.

White House Redux competition

Selection process by competition
jury. The White House Redux ideas
competition was organised by
Storefront for Art and Architecture:
'What if the White House, the ultimate
architectural symbol of political
power, were to be designed today?'
The competition attracted almost 500
entries from 42 countries.

Introduction

This chapter places architectural design in its familiar context: the design studio. This is where the creative work happens; it is an environment common to both architectural education and the profession. It is a place of practical things; a place of production containing equipment for making models, for drawing digitally and by hand. It is often supported by specialised workshops and printing facilities. Resources for research, such as architectural books and journals, will also be on hand.

The studio has its own culture: it is a place where research, experimentation, discussion and the testing of ideas can take place before they are put into action on site. The gathering together of like-minded colleagues capable of collaboration and constructive criticism assists the development of architectural proposals and the fostering of mutual preoccupations.

Design studio, NL Architects

This photograph taken at NL Architects' office shows a scene common to both professional and student design studios, with flexible shared working space equipped for drawing, making and collaboration.

'I think we believe very strongly in the discussion forum culture of the studio compared to what you might call an office. So everyone has the same chair and everyone has the same desk. Everything is open and everyone has access to everything. Everyone's opinion is aired. I like that and I like to be able to talk to and reach everybody. I wouldn't like to be in a separate place at all. If I want a separate place I just go for a walk.'
John Tuomey, O'Donnell + Tuomey Architects

Historically the link between a drawing and the execution of that drawing on site, were much closer in time and place than they are today. A mason might mark out a design on a piece of stone immediately prior to cutting it directly on site. The design studio has evolved as a place that enables design to be developed both far away and far in advance of its actual implementation.

This separation has obvious advantages: it gives the opportunity to consider the coherence of the whole scheme prior to construction; and disadvantages: it is easy to make mistakes through the miscommunication of information between the office and the site. However, one unexpected outcome is the emergence of a studio culture within the design studio.

This culture is so strong that it was absorbed by architectural education when it, too, became separated from practice. This disconnection has led to tensions between education and practice. Typically offices demand practice-ready architects who are able to slot seamlessly into a particular working method, and higher education insists on retaining its mandate to educate progressive graduates willing to challenge the status quo. However, design-studio culture is common to both education and practice and architects must be conscious of this link. The culture of architecture should remain relevant to education, practice and, above all, to the changing world outside.

Emergence in practice

An early example of a vibrant design studio culture is one that emerged in Britain in the 17th century, in the Office of Works under Sir Christopher Wren. The Restoration of the Monarchy in 1661, followed closely by the Great Fire of London in 1666, meant an extensive building programme for the church, monarchy and state. This was a huge undertaking for Wren and it was necessary for him to delegate the design and management of projects to fellow professionals. The Office of Works developed a studio culture of coherent working methods and a shared theory of architecture. Communication of this culture between members allowed its dialogue to develop to a degree of sophistication that was much more difficult for individual master masons or gentlemen architects to achieve.

Wells Cathedral Stonemasons

An apprentice stonemason at Wells Cathedral, UK, tracing a design on to stone prior to cutting. Stonemasons still use the ancient apprentice system to learn their skills on site.

The design studio

Bourges Cathedral

Survey by John Harvey of stone
tracery sketched by masons directly
on to the floor of Bourges Cathedral,
France, in the 12th century. The
term tracery may come from the
'tracing floors' on which the complex
patterns of late Gothic windows were
laid out before being lifted into place.

Wren was a particularly skilled collaborator and created
a long-standing and successful working relationship
with several architects in his office, in particular Nicholas
Hawksmoor. Hawksmoor rose from the position of clerk to
architect and worked with Wren on projects such as St Paul's
Cathedral. He had benefited from, and contributed to,
a design studio that was a place of learning and teaching.

The Bauhaus: preliminary course

Bauhaus Preliminary Course, 1922

The three colours black, white and red in four proportion patterns: three-division, arithmetic progression, geometrical progression and golden section. Gouache on paper by Ludwig Hirschfeld-Mack.

Bauhaus Preliminary Course, 1930

Suggesting space through the arrangement of rectangles and letters by Georg Neidenberger.

This case study describes the teaching at the Bauhaus school, which was established in Weimar, Germany in 1919. Its mission was not only to reform art and architecture education but to change society by doing so. The school's radical teachers and innovative teaching methods were hugely influential. The illustrated exercises carried out by Bauhaus students have been chosen for their focus on spatial experimentation with line, colour and form.

Student work

Students joining the Bauhaus were required to complete a Preliminary Course (*vorkurs*) founded by Johannes Itten. He designed a system to establish the creative potential of students and provide a thorough basis in visual and creative theory.

Itten's approach embraced both intuition and method. His wish for educational reform and involvement with the artistic avant-garde led him to encourage students to analyse and invent rather than to learn by copying, as was usual in contemporary art schools. Itten was a charismatic teacher, even persuading several students to follow his unconventional religious beliefs and modes of dress and diet. He believed in the emotional and spiritual qualities of colour and saw colour and form as being inseparable. Students were to focus on the most basic geometric shapes and colours to promote their understanding and clear communication of these qualities. Itten's student exercises were designed to explore the contrast between different colours and shapes in as many ways as possible, both two- and three-dimensionally.

Wassily Kandinsky and Paul Klee were also influential teachers on the Preliminary Course. Kandinsky explored the relationship between the warmth and tone of colour. He related colour and form to each other and also to the drawing plane. This demonstrated the spatial effects of colour and form. Line was considered as a point in motion; the force used to create it attributing qualities to the line. Klee considered the artistic process to be mysterious but that the basic skills needed for expression could be taught.

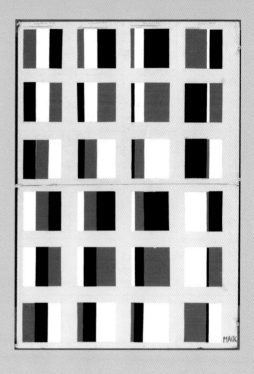

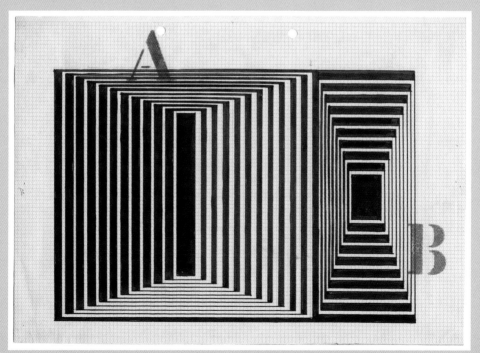

As the complexity and cultural prominence of architectural projects increased, so did the recognition and status of the architect. As the training of architects became more formal, design studio culture was transformed from a professional to an educational context.

Early architectural education

In the 19th century some architects wished to achieve the respectability of professional status. In the UK, in 1831, a Royal Charter awarded the title of architect to professionals, and membership of the Royal Institute of British Architects began. Such privilege also brought responsibility and so more structure and formality was introduced into architectural training. Learning as an apprentice within a professional environment inevitably fostered a mentoring or 'master/pupil' relationship and this was often translated in a very literal way as higher education began to develop.

In 1847 the Architectural Association became the first institution in the UK to offer a structured programme of instruction. As more schools were established, the previous system of apprenticeships or articled pupillage declined, until by the 1920s most trainee architects received formal training at an institution of higher education.

After the First World War, revolutionary times called for a revolution in architecture and the Bauhaus art school exemplified this approach (see pages 12–13). The founding manifesto and programme for the school under its first director, Walter Gropius, stated that art cannot be taught but that craft and manual skill could be. Students would once again learn by doing. Value and status were restored to those undertaking this less 'academic' approach. They would reach back to the idea of apprenticeships and focus on the experience of making in the school's workshops, under the supervision of the skilled studio masters.

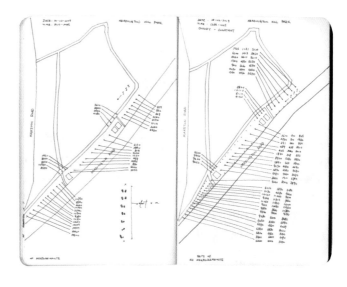

Sketchbook

This sketchbook page, by U leong To, illustrates the analysis of sound on site. A sketchbook records the progress and process of a project, and it is the process of architectural design that students of architecture are engaged in learning. In addition to sketches, diagrams, notes, site information, precedent images and trial pieces for the project itself, a sketchbook may also contain ideas for other (sometimes future) projects and is a place to record sources of general inspiration such as quotations, work seen at exhibitions, on field trips and while travelling.

Architectural education today

Today the design studio is central to most systems of architectural education and practice. Learning to design has much in common with other practical arts, such as learning to play an instrument. The more you practise, the better you get. The act of learning by doing gives you instant feedback in terms of the visual and physical result and this allows you to do it better the next time. Just as music students rehearse for a big concert, architecture students working on a project in the studio are getting ready for their first commission. Student projects are rarely truly 'live' in the way that professional projects are, but normally have some element of reality embedded in them.

The legacy of apprenticeships and the old master/pupil relationships that previously existed in the training of architects have had an influence on the structure of architectural education today. During every design project, students are assigned to a design-studio tutor, to give them the opportunity to learn from a range of architects and their different approaches to design.

Can architectural design be taught?

There are elements of architectural education that retain some mystery for both students and tutors. The design studio, the role of the design-studio tutor and crits, also known as reviews – all are ubiquitous and carefully protected despite the fact that, although they seem to work, nobody appears to agree on why or how, or whether they could be replaced by something better. While it could be argued that it is possible to learn how to become an architect, there are doubts whether art (and by extension, parts of architectural design), can be taught. The essential problem is, how can you teach someone to generate 'great' architecture and how do you teach someone to find 'inspiration'?

In his book *Why Art Cannot Be Taught*, James Elkins defines six different answers to this question. To read them, substitute the word 'architecture' for the word 'art':

1 Art can be taught, but nobody knows quite how.

2 Art can be taught, but it seems as if it can't be since so few students become outstanding artists.

3 Art cannot be taught, but it can be fostered or helped along.

4 Art cannot be taught or even nourished, but it is possible to teach right up to the beginnings of art, so that students are ready to make art the moment they graduate.

5 Great art cannot be taught, but more run-of-the-mill art can.

6 Art cannot be taught, but neither can anything else.

Like art, architecture is always searching for greatness among its ranks and can never satisfactorily define the reasons for, or moment behind, inspiration. This need not undermine the exercise of architectural education, however. In fact, this struggle fuels the constant reinvention of both architectural education and practice.

Ways of learning

Despite the debate, architecture continues to be 'taught'. Some schools operate a system where everyone learns together in a year group, following the same project briefs, supported by a team of tutors. Other schools adopt a unit system, where students are assigned to a smaller unit, which will explicitly follow a process or brief that relates to the skills, methods, preoccupations and agenda of the unit tutor. These units are often 'vertical' with different year groups learning together. Everyone in the studio will follow a similar journey, all getting to different answers.

Group tutorials are an opportunity to learn from fellow students as well as tutors, by discussing and debating common themes. They are also an opportunity to test how well design work communicates to others in an informal setting. A typical individual tutorial will involve exchanging a lot of information and ideas; reflecting on the work; exercising critical judgement; exploring a particular focus on the design; challenging the brief and so on. It is similar in many ways to a client meeting or to a progress review with a colleague in the office.

Workshops are important events in the studio. These short, intensive studio teaching sessions involve following a task that relates to a particular stage in a given project. This is carefully focused and designed to equip students with a new skill or way of working that will push their design on to the next stage. In Chapter 3 there are short technique sections that are derived from studio workshops.

'The reviews added focus to my project, forcing me to take a step back and understand my concepts so that I could articulate them clearly to others. This is also the ultimate sanity check; you want to make sure your project is watertight and will stand up to questioning.'
Will Fisher, architectural student, Oxford Brookes University

Assessment

Reviews, also known as crits, happen at various stages of a project. These are normally either informal pin-ups or formal interim and final reviews. The format is flexible and capable of taking many forms. However, the most common is for students to pin up their work, display their models and present their work verbally to a panel of reviewers and students. It is important to plan a convincing verbal presentation in order to communicate the project fully in the time allocated.

In a formal review, you may be asked to provide written comments reflecting on the review and will often be given written feedback and/or formal assessment afterwards. Designers need to be skilled in making critical judgements in order to make design decisions and reviews are a way to reveal the reasoning behind reviewers' judgements, allowing you to develop your own critical judgement. Different architects will voice contradictory opinions about the same piece of work and the discussion helps everyone to explore the reasons behind this.

It is especially important to be well rested the night before a review to be in the best frame of mind to view work objectively and to learn from the techniques and ideas of peers. It can be difficult to be on the receiving end of criticism, especially after putting so much thought and effort into a project; however, even the best project can still be improved upon. Feedback will focus on evaluation, the identification of areas to be improved and suggestions for how this could be achieved.

Interpretation of some common terms used by architects during crits

Critic	Unresolved
Meaning	Needs more work

Critic	Interesting
Meaning	Strange (not fatally flawed but certainly not making sense yet. I don't want to de-rail your progress though)

Critic	Consider
Meaning	Needs more thought: try this possible solution/ direction...

Critic	Powerful
Meaning	A very good idea expressed in a compelling way

Critic	Inventive
Meaning	I wish I'd thought of that!

The design studio

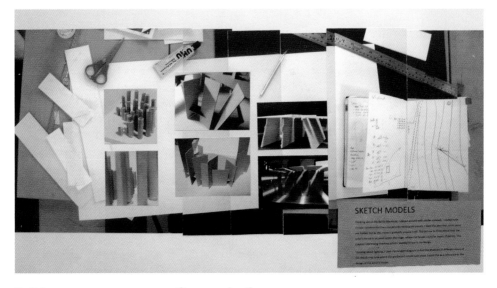

SKETCH MODELS

Portfolio

A portfolio is an important record, not only of the resolved project but also the development process. This portfolio page, by Farah Yusof, shows the processes and tools employed in making a series of sketch models, and a sketchbook page that records the thought process behind the sketch models.

Communication

Portfolio reviews or interviews are used by many schools to arrive at a final assessment of design work. In some schools the student will not be present when their work is being assessed. This is a good test of graphical communication skills because images and text must be carefully considered in order to explain a complex project concisely, occasionally to assessors who may be unfamiliar with the project. Both the design development process (sketchbooks, sketch designs, sketch models and analysis) and the finished product (final drawings, photographs of models and reports) will be included. At the end of the year, most schools put on an exhibition of student work. Opportunities for publicity and disseminating their work are essential for architects. The end-of-year show is an important opportunity for students to gain experience in creating an exhibition.

Architectural Association: student pavilions

The Architectural Association holds an annual Projects Review exhibition at the end of the academic year. This provides an opportunity for the school to display their students' work and connect to the wider profession. This case study documents some of the recent pavilions designed, built and exhibited by the Architectural Association at the Projects Review.

The projects

Between 2006 and 2009, second- and third-year students in Intermediate Unit 2 built a series of pavilions in the square outside the Architectural Association. The projects were developed over the course of the academic year. Students were encouraged to contribute an idea every time the group met to progress the design. The most successful proposals were shortlisted for more detailed development, with students working in small groups to explore the viability of each option. Eventually one design was chosen to be progressed towards construction. Testing and construction of the project involved the whole unit and tutors collaborating in a manner similar to an architectural office, with consultant engineers, material specialists and technicians giving expert advice.

The brief for the pavilions keeps the programmatic requirements relatively simple. Function is not prescribed beyond the pavilion's role as a focal point and space enclosure. Shelter and seating provision are not prerequisites. This looseness allows the designer to focus on their own preoccupations and conceptual direction. They also explored the possibilities of emerging digital design and manufacturing techniques, and the potential of innovative timber construction. Live student projects are excellent ways to push the boundaries of what is considered possible because educational environments can sometimes offer the time and freedom to experiment and explore solutions that may be dismissed as inefficient or risky in a professional environment.

**Driftwood Pavilion by
Danacia Sibingo and Intermediate
Unit 2, 2009**

The Intermediate Unit 2 pavilions have used innovative materials such as Kerto, a lightweight laminated veneer lumber (LVL) in different configurations and forms according to the design of each pavilion. In addition to physical models and prototypes, they have used digital modelling to design and manufacture via Computer Integrated Manufacturing (CIM) techniques.

Driftwood Pavilion was inspired by the unit's interest in the idea of motion and the eroded rock formations and architecture of the Jordanian city of Petra. It provides a semi-enclosed space surrounded by an undulating and contoured timber wall of varying thickness and with occasional openings. It is constructed from 28 layers of 4mm-thick bent plywood on a spruce sub-frame. The team generated 112 technical drawings in order to manufacture and construct the pavilion.

Swoosh Pavilion by Valeria García Abarca and Intermediate Unit 2, 2008

Swoosh Pavilion is an open-latticed structure that curves and twists around the square's lamp-posts to form canopies, openings and benches. The design allows people to use it in several different ways at once: to meet, sit, rest and eat. The dynamic form and open structure create an array of shadow patterns on the ground beside the pavilion. The structure is formed from 653 pieces of laminated veneer lumber that were shaped by a CNC milling machine. The white stain applied to the timber emphasises the difference between the structure and its shadow. The main vertical curved columns are connected by shorter, slimmer cross beams that radiate out from the centre. The whole structure was bolted together to ease its construction and dismantling. It sits on two heavy steel bases that counter-balance the cantilevering timber.

Bad Hair Pavilion by Margaret Dewhurst and Intermediate Unit 2, 2007

Bad Hair Pavilion was inspired by the designer's interpretation of her own wet hair as it dried. The pavilion rises into a dome and falls to drape on to the ground making places to sit and lie down. Although the structure looks tangled, with its complicated double-curved, twisted glue-laminated beams, there is order to the structure and construction. The outer two layers are freer while the inner two layers are more geometric. The timber has been stained a rich brown and the members are bolted together.

To celebrate the tenth anniversary of the Architectural Association's Design Research Lab (DRL 10), existing and graduate students were invited to compete to design a pavilion. Alan Dempsey and Alvin Huang were invited to develop and construct their design for a glass-fibre reinforced concrete structure. This material is normally used for cladding rather than structural purposes. Their ambitious design required extensive prototyping and material testing. The resulting pavilion uses 13mm thick panels to provide the structure, skin, walls, floor and furniture of the pavilion.

Architectural education › Architectural Association: student pavilions › Design studio projects

Every design studio project is different. What follows is an attempt to introduce the concept of project work and to describe the characteristics of a typical project. Many student project briefs will emphasise particular stages of the project over others in order to teach those areas in more detail. Some projects may even remove stages that are not relevant to the aims of the exercise.

Starting a design project

A typical design studio project begins with a research, experimentation and analysis phase to understand the problems set by the brief: surveying the site, sketching, interviewing clients and users, mapping and analysing the site. The project may be real, based on reality or entirely imagined. The brief may even be open, requiring the student to complete it, to identify a site, client or building type(s). The brief is normally designed to allow students to develop their own interests and build upon those of the tutor. There will often be elements of group work and cooperation at this point to accelerate the group's knowledge and understanding at a time when much research is needed.

While absorbing all of this information, students will be exploring multiple ideas and potential solutions to the design problem through preliminary sketches, diagrams and sketch models. Different ideas need to be explored and tested out. Tutors often assist with the generation and direction of ideas by running design workshops, group tutorials and pin-ups for discussion of ideas, as well as lectures and building visits.

Project: Oxford Literary Festival
Location: Oxford, UK
Designer: Joanna Gorringe Minto
Date: 2010

This early sketch model/drawing was made at the beginning of a project. It expresses the idea of a tunnel with an open structure and patterned cladding emerging from the landscape and casting shadows upon it.

'There are two ingredients when one is starting any project. One is an understanding of the brief and one is an understanding of the site. Strangely enough the relationship of the project with its site often outlives the relationship of the project with the programme and certainly always outlives the relationship of the project with the client.'
John Tuomey, O'Donnell + Tuomey Architects

Developing a design project

Once the design problem has been understood and restated, the designer will begin to make decisions on the focus and direction of the project. Experimentation and testing through drawings and models continue but these should become more defined. This definition often arises from a decision by the designer to focus on a few particular issues each time; for example, entrance to the site, relevant local social issues, how to build with a particular material.

During the design development phase ideas are refined, decisions made and complexity increased. Drawings and models explore the proposal in part and as a whole, moving back and forth between the general and the particular. This may lead to a questioning of decisions made in the earlier phases and often requires a return to an earlier stage to make changes before moving on again. At various stages along the way judgements need to be made about how to represent and communicate the work. Learning new skills and how to use new tools will help support and develop the design work. No two architects follow exactly the same path. It is quite usual to jump between stages and to deliberately return to others. It is very normal, necessary even, to get stuck and make mistakes that can be learned from. It is important for you to breathe life into the project and contribute to its direction by participating in the debate going on in the design studio.

Professional design projects

Projects in a professional environment follow a broadly similar rhythm to student projects with early analytical and experimental phases, the development of the brief with the client and preliminary sketch designs developing into more resolved proposals. Regular client presentations and design reviews with colleagues in the office are similar to crits.

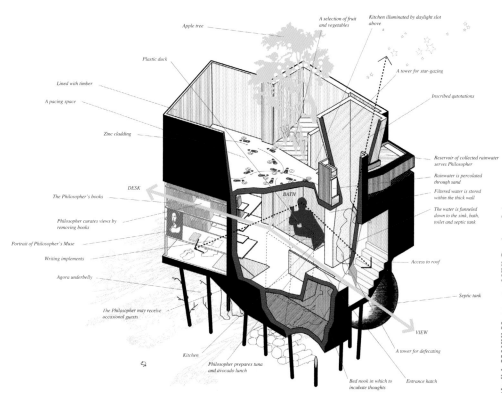

A selection of fruit and vegetables

Kitchen illuminated by daylight slot above

Apple tree

Plastic duck

A tower for star-gazing

Lined with timber

Inscribed quotations

A pacing space

Zinc cladding

Reservoir of collected rainwater serves Philosopher

Rainwater is percolated through sand

DESK

Filtered water is stored within the thick wall

The Philosopher's books

BATH

The water is funneled down to the sink, bath, toilet and septic tank

Philosopher curates views by removing books

Portrait of Philosopher's Muse

Writing implements

Access to roof

Agora underbelly

Septic tank

The Philosopher may receive occasional guests

VIEW

A tower for defecating

Kitchen

Philosopher prepares tuna and avocado lunch

Bed nook in which to incubate thoughts

Entrance hatch

Project: House for a Philosopher
Location: UK
Architect: AOC
Date 2006

This cutaway axonometric describes the design for 'a simple house to stimulate different modes of thinking'.

The most significant differences from student projects are the negotiations and applications for approval by planning authorities at scheme design stage and building control at detailed design stage, as well as the production of information for tender, where drawings are priced by contractors who bid for the work. Throughout the project, the architect coordinates the contributions of various consultants, such as engineers. The management of the project on site is a significant part of the architect's role but this is experienced by few students while in full-time education. There is still a need for architectural decisions, and therefore design work, while construction is in progress.

Architectural Association: student pavilions › **Design studio projects** › Zaha Hadid: MAXXI Museum of XXI Century Arts

Conceptual sketch drawn in
notebook

In 1997 Zaha Hadid Architects won the competition to design the MAXXI Museum of XXI Century Arts in Rome. The construction of an ambitious design for a new museum, in a city of glorious historic museums, was culturally and politically significant and the project developed slowly over a number of years. This case study looks at different stages in its development.

The project

In an early sketch from Zaha Hadid's notebook (shown above) it is possible to understand the importance of the fluid parallel and crossing lines that would become characteristic of the constructed MAXXI building. Hadid has referred to them as 'streams'. The sketch carries with it some of the ideas on flow and movement within the city that are found in much of Hadid's work. At this early stage, these lines may express the whole city, the building itself or both. Such sketches may not always be project specific: they express ideas and possibilities rather than certainties and solutions.

The design studio

Conceptual painting

The painting above brings the design thinking towards representation of form and its location within the city. Although the image is still very open and abstract, the three-dimensional context of the site is more evident. The existing urban grain and river are represented and a small outline proposal for the building is shown sitting loosely within that context. The parallel and crossing 'streams' of the building are shown in more resolved detail at a bigger scale and the layering of these streams is expressed. At this stage, paintings and three-dimensional modelling are not intended to be literally translated into architecture, they are diagrams and images of what the building could be.

Photograph taken during construction

When the architect considers the building at full scale, they must tackle another level of detail, complexity and design. What could be legitimately represented as seamless and flowing when represented at a small scale, as if viewed from a distance, must be designed to cope with the junctions between elements and the texture of materials when experienced at close hand.

The photograph above, taken during construction, still bears a resemblance to the earlier conceptual painting and sketch. The complexity of reality is also revealed. The building has a richer palette of materials; the process of construction and the immediacy of the surrounding context are evident. The transient qualities of the site, so difficult to represent in architectural drawings, are immediately obvious: variations in light conditions, growth of vegetation, and the expectation of future change are tangible.

The building replaces former low-rise military barracks and is set outside the city centre in a residential area. MAXXI is horizontal in direction. Its criss-crossing layers respect,

Public view of building prior to exhibition installation

rediscover and create the complex circulation patterns of the city, its inhabitants and their buildings. Further campus buildings are yet to be constructed in order to complete this composition.

The movement around the building exterior translates into the building itself. Hadid has described the way to experience the contemporary artworks as a 'drift' through the galleries. Rather than a series of cellular rooms, the visitor's route is linear, with moments to choose alternative routes and enter galleries at different points. The two long walls defining the galleries intersect and separate the space. The 'streams' that were visible from the first sketch survive as deep-ribbed roof members, visible both internally and externally. These modulate the light admitted into the gallery and will be used to hang flexible exhibition dividers. The strong black forms of the stairways and balustrades are reminiscent of the confident movement lines of that initial sketch.

The principle behind design-studio projects in education is that of 'learning by doing'. It is a practical way to test and strengthen design skills and an immediate way to reinforce what is being learned.

The problem with this method is that it can be difficult for you to predict what you need to learn. For example, you may wish to develop the internal space of a building but are not sure whether it should follow the external form, burst out of it or express an entirely different form. What is the right answer? You may imagine a few possibilities to explore that seem in tune with the concept so far. This seems like a very inefficient way of doing things: surely one answer must be better than another. Probably, but you will only find out by trying them. Once you have explored and begun to commit to certain directions, this will lead you to make subsequent moves in related directions.

If there is no such thing as one right answer to any architectural problem, how do architects make decisions about the right answer for their project? Knowledge gained from past experience is certainly one part of the solution. However, the architect must also use their critical judgement. At this point, the individual's value system helps them to distinguish between competing demands: a beautiful and radical 'object-building' may galvanise civic pride and stimulate local regeneration but possible risks associated with innovative construction methods may undermine the client's confidence to proceed with the project.

Publicity, feedback, criticism, dialogue and the sharing of ideas are absolutely essential to architecture. They provide a control mechanism for the quality and direction of unbuilt work and proposals. They also maintain the debate about what architecture could and should be. There will never be consensus. On visiting different architects' offices and architecture schools it is clear that they are tremendously diverse. Every design studio has its own sub-culture but this is still linked, however tenuously, to the rest of the profession.

Year one group tutorial

Sketch drawn for the PAL
(Peer Assisted Learning) project
undertaken by Justus Van Der Hoven
and Jamie Williamson. This sketch
of a group tutorial shows the hands-
on participatory nature of the design
studio, with students discussing the
development of a prototype that they
are making with a tutor. The tutorial
is a loosely structured discussion
involving questions and answers
passed freely between tutor and
student until both parties reach
agreement on the progress and
direction of the project. Students
not directly involved can either work
in the studio while the tutorial is in
progress or join in if they wish.

This exploration of teaching, learning and practising in the
design studio has begun to reveal that architects are required
to participate and contribute to the life and direction of the
studio in order to make it work and also to benefit from
what it has to offer. At its most positive, involvement gives
opportunities to learn, find inspiration, participate in current
debate and opinion and be informed on the latest advances
in design, methods, tools and skills. It can also lead to
recognition by peers and, by implication, advancement in
the profession. At its worst this culture can become self-
referential, clubby, exclusive and even irrelevant to the rest
of the world. Architects must use their critical judgement and
exploit their capacity for reinvention to ensure that design-
studio culture remains fluid, positive, accessible and relevant.

Project: Hearth House
Location: London, UK
Architect: AOC
Date: 2010

This drawing, named a 'Spatial Constitution' by the architects, represents all of the significant activities that they hope their clients will engage in while living in the house.

This chapter describes the cerebral process of design and the skills needed to implement design ideas and develop as an architectural designer.

Architectural design problems are complex and require creative solutions. Although architects often make provocative, didactic or stylistic judgements about different forms of architecture that they either value or deride, there is not one 'correct' way to design. Architectural experiences, influences and inspirational tutors or colleagues contribute towards the making of an architect but each person responds differently to these stimuli and must make their own value judgements. Ultimately, the moment of design springs from the individual imagination, no matter how collaborative the circumstances that provoked it.

This chapter attempts to define experiences and skills that are common to all architects engaged in the design process and to give substance to some of the more cerebral and intangible qualities of architectural design. The better the architect understands their actions, the greater their freedom to develop and explore the different possibilities inherent in their own design process.

Architectural design requires the solution of complex problems. This is central to an understanding of the design methods, processes and approaches that are discussed later in this chapter.

Understanding complex problems

No matter how similar their training and experience, no two architects working alone will ever produce an identical architectural proposal, even if those two architects are deeply sympathetic to each other's ideas and have worked together for their entire career. However, they will be able to recognise the other's work because of the familiar ideas and the way that they are expressed. In this respect the moment of design can be seen as an individual act. This is where the complexity of the task must be broken down and understood internally in the mind of the individual and their interpretation of the problem expressed.

Design does not just require the solution of complex problems but relies on the individual to identify, state or define the design problem. This requires an enhanced ability not only to perceive the problem, but also to focus on particular problems as being the most relevant to solve. Architects must develop their perception and critical judgement as essential skills.

This tolerance of multiple solutions in architecture seems to contrast greatly with other disciplines, such as science, where there is a drive to search for evidence to prove that one particular theory is correct. However, there is no doubt that scientific problems are also incredibly complex. Why do architects insist on 'bespoke' solutions and methods rather than working together to research and agree on one single optimum, or even correct, answer to questions such as, 'What are the qualities of the "ideal" house?'

Multiple solutions

There is no such thing as one right answer in architecture.

In his book *Tools for Ideas: An Introduction to Architectural Design,* Christian Gänshirt contrasts scientific thought and method to that of architecture. He refers to Horst Rittel's definition of 'tricky or wicked' problems, which have no definitive solution. There may only be one opportunity to provide a solution (because the next time the problem will be different; in architecture there will be a different site, brief, budget or client) and so it is impossible to definitively compare the quality of that solution with another. In addition, if an architect made a comprehensive study of every option available for every small decision in order to solve the bigger problem, there would be no time to act. The benefit of action far outweighs the negligible benefit associated with certainty on the multiplicity of smaller questions.

For an architect, the imperative to act is the justification of their existence. To compound this, the knowledge that there is no means of establishing one right answer drives the architect to adjust their process in the endless search to improve upon the last project and explore another idea that presents itself as imperative. This leads to an empirical approach to solving architectural problems.

'It's delicate. We don't force whatever's emerging. On the contrary, we try to keep it in peripheral vision for as long as possible and try to let it acquire its own qualities and its own momentum. It's such a delicate thing and if you try and lock it down into a crude, over-presented way, that is an absolute anathema to the way that we work.'

Steve Tompkins, Haworth Tompkins

Problem solving › NL Architects: Prisma housing

Critical judgement

There is one particular device that the architect uses to counteract the absence of one right answer in architecture. This is the ability to make critical judgements. Critical judgement is a term much used in architecture schools. It should not be confused with 'criticism': the comments made by reviewers at crits or reviews.

Critical judgement is a way of thinking; it helps architects to make decisions about how to solve architectural problems. It is the ability of an architect to question their own decisions willingly and openly and compare them to the other possible decisions that they, or their collaborators, can imagine.

Critical judgement is a product of an architect's core values, knowledge, training, experience, aesthetic preferences and current thought. It is reflective, reactive, contextual and pragmatic. The difficulty with critical judgement as a method for decision making is that it is not a transparent process and is only as good as the individual architect, their imagination and their ability to learn from their mistakes.

The strength of critical judgement as a method is its ability to adapt to the ever-changing nature of any given architectural problem. This flexible thinking fosters lateral thought, which is essential for creativity. It also gives architects the will to question existing ideas; to challenge the project brief or status quo. It is an essential function of the architect to ask fundamental questions, however awkward, because a flawed solution to a complex architectural problem will cement new, unanticipated problems into its execution. In short, it is far better to ask difficult questions at the beginning of the design process than to build your mistakes.

Architectural language: some commonly used architectural terms explained

Architecture:	**Aperture**		Architecture:	**Space**	
English:	Window		English:	Room	
Meaning:	An opening (the design is not sufficiently resolved to be able to distinguish between windows, doors and other openings yet).		Meaning:	The quality/form/function of the space should be further considered before it is named as a particular type of room or space.	

It is important to ask how critical judgement is learned, because it is a technique so central to architectural design. The answer is not an easy one. As with much architectural education, there is a strong element of learning by doing and less evidence of instructive forms of teaching. You may find that it simply becomes necessary to make a choice between several promising ideas and the deadline normally compels you to make a decision. However, it is important not to become rigid in your thinking, always opting for the first solution. Tutorials offer an opportunity for you to reason through the decisions made. Critical judgement is primarily verbal and you should become skilled in 'architectural language' to understand and participate.

'I know that I become very impatient about speed once we know where we're going. So it is a very dilatory sort of a process where you orbit the thing and actually, you often try to avoid it for as long as possible, and then you can't avoid it any longer, and then you pounce, and after that you want it done as fast as possible.'

John Tuomey, O'Donnell + Tuomey

Architecture:	**Plane/envelope**
English:	Floor, wall, roof
Meaning:	It is too early to fix the form by naming a surface as vertical, horizontal or inclined.

Architecture:	**Describe the materiality of your proposal**
English:	What is it made from?
Meaning:	Don't just assume 'brick' if your drawing suggests a light, delicate structure.

Architecture:	**Describe the scale of your proposal**
English:	How big is it?
Meaning:	How do the proportions of the building relate to the occupants and the context (rural or urban)?

Making and reflecting

Nothing is genuinely fixed or real until the building is constructed. Therefore, the design possibilities can seem endless. The architect needs to find ways to simulate or represent their ideas and proposals; such as drawing or modelling, for example. The different tools that can be used to communicate ideas have their own varying qualities. For example, clay is mouldable and can be used to create fluid external forms, but it is also heavy and unsuitable for creating internal spaces or slender shells. Design decisions are being made in a constant feedback loop while the drawing or model is being crafted. These decisions are influenced by the tool or media being used. Designers benefit from the creative possibilities of craft and the act of making; ideas can be sparked by 'happy accidents'. It is important to have a broad range of craft skills and to understand the limitations and possibilities of each design tool.

Every architect follows an iterative cycle of making, followed by reflecting, followed by making again. Making and reflecting will enable you to acknowledge the possibilities and limitations of your own design process – and therefore become a better designer – and also to test out the effectiveness of your proposed design solutions.

Diagram by Christian Gänshirt

Tools influence the process and product of expression of an idea and therefore our perception of it. The designer will reflect upon the result and be influenced by this to further develop their ideas. Gänshirt suggests that design is a complex activity that is difficult to define but it 'can also be approached and described by means of the tools and cultural techniques deployed in the design process. Looking at it from this point of view helps achieve an appropriate degree of detachment from personal working methods, and makes it possible to see the fundamental relations between individual activities.'

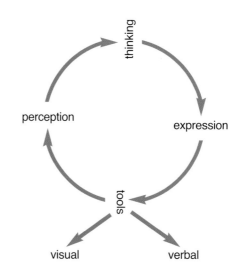

thinking

perception

expression

tools

visual   verbal

The design process

Restrictions

Critical discussion in practice occurs within the design studio and between clients and other interested parties such as planners, building users, heritage groups and politicians. These bodies throw hitherto unexpected restrictions and opportunities into the design process, which are rarely encountered in education. However, the flexibility of an empirical design process and the familiarity with the possibilities of multiple solutions should equip the architect to take a creative approach to such situations.

Architects often describe restrictions and the requirements of a brief, site and client as examples of positive generators for design. Many would say that they need restrictions in order to design. The apparently unwelcome restriction tethers infinite possibilities to a fixed point of reality, however mundane. This demands a solution to a real problem that cannot be ignored and so the design activity begins to work on the restriction until it becomes something positive.

For example, fire escape regulations may impose conditions on the means of escape and therefore circulation of a building. A good architect could use this as an opportunity to design communal circulation spaces of real quality where people will take pleasure in meeting on the way to their otherwise isolated cellular offices.

Architecture seeks to fulfil a need or purpose; to have a function. The willingness of architects to use their critical judgement and creativity to challenge assumptions, coupled with the freedom of knowing that there is no one right answer, means even the most difficult design problems are seen as an opportunity for creative thought.

'It's not real. You're not drawing the real thing. You're drawing something that gets you to the real thing.'
Graham Haworth, Haworth Tompkins

Problem solving › NL Architects: Prisma housing

NL Architects: Prisma housing

Name: Prisma
Completed: 2010
Client: Stichting
De Huismeesters,
Ed Moonen/Roelof Jong
Location: Groningen,
The Netherlands
Programme:
52 apartments and nursery
with consultation office
Height: 16 floors
Gross floor area: 8,650m^2

bottom right:
Diagram: balconies
___

This diagram explains the factors
influencing the development of the
form. The building stacks the largest
apartment types at the bottom and
the smaller ones above. Balconies
wrap around this stepped form, tying
it together. They are cut away to
maximise views and solar orientation.
They also vary in depth and length
to suit the type of apartment that
they serve. The proportions, form
and pattern produced by this
design process are controlled by
the architect, whose response is
both practical (logical) and aesthetic
(intuitive).

**NL Architects is an Amsterdam-based office opened in
1997 and run by its three principals Pieter Bannenberg,
Walter van Dijk and Kamiel Klaasse. This case study
illustrates their approach to working with the restrictions
of a brief and their use of diagrams and models to
explore, test and record possible design solutions.**

The project

NL Architects' interest in everyday life does not lead them
towards mundane solutions for insignificant problems.
In fact, they are concerned with large issues that affect
everyone, such as how to improve human interaction within
the city. To achieve this they employ a design process
that plays with the restrictions of the brief until they create
something quite unexpected. Their apparently obedient and
relentless re-working of the permutations possible within the
brief leads to answers that are surprising and original.

Prisma is located within a post-Second World War housing
development of largely mid-rise apartments and open public
space. Much of the existing housing is considered sub-
standard for future needs. NL Architects' topographical study
revealed that the original building, although in need of
renovation, has the distinction of being a rare, high-rise
element within a flat landscape. The excellent vistas from the
flats to landmarks beyond led to an idea to focus the design
on creating new balconies, which would further exploit this.
The balconies would also provide a fresh new skin to the
existing exterior. Many different permutations were tried for
these balconies, using models and diagrams, which explored
issues such as variations and locations of apartment types,
silhouette, volume, privacy for occupants, dynamic form,
maintenance access, equity of exterior space for occupants
and orientation towards the sun.

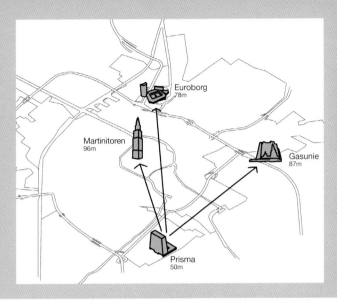

Diagram: vista

Study of topography and views
in a flat landscape with low-rise
development. NL Architects make
skillful intuitive leaps and use
analytical diagrams or graphics
to explain their design process and
the conceptual thinking behind the
generation of architectural form.

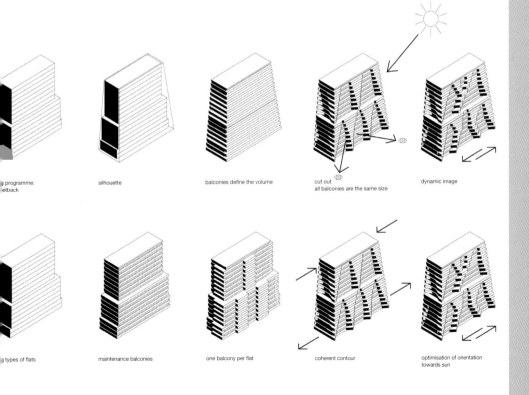

programme: setback	silhouette	balconies define the volume	cut out / all balconies are the same size	dynamic image
types of flats	maintenance balconies	one balcony per flat	coherent contour	optimisation of orientation towards sun

Sketch models

Sequence of sketch models
showing the development of the
design. The form of the exterior
changed in response to analysis
of sun paths and views of the
surrounding area, development
of different apartment types and
studies of privacy for residents
using the balconies.

right:
Prisma

View of completed building.

The design process

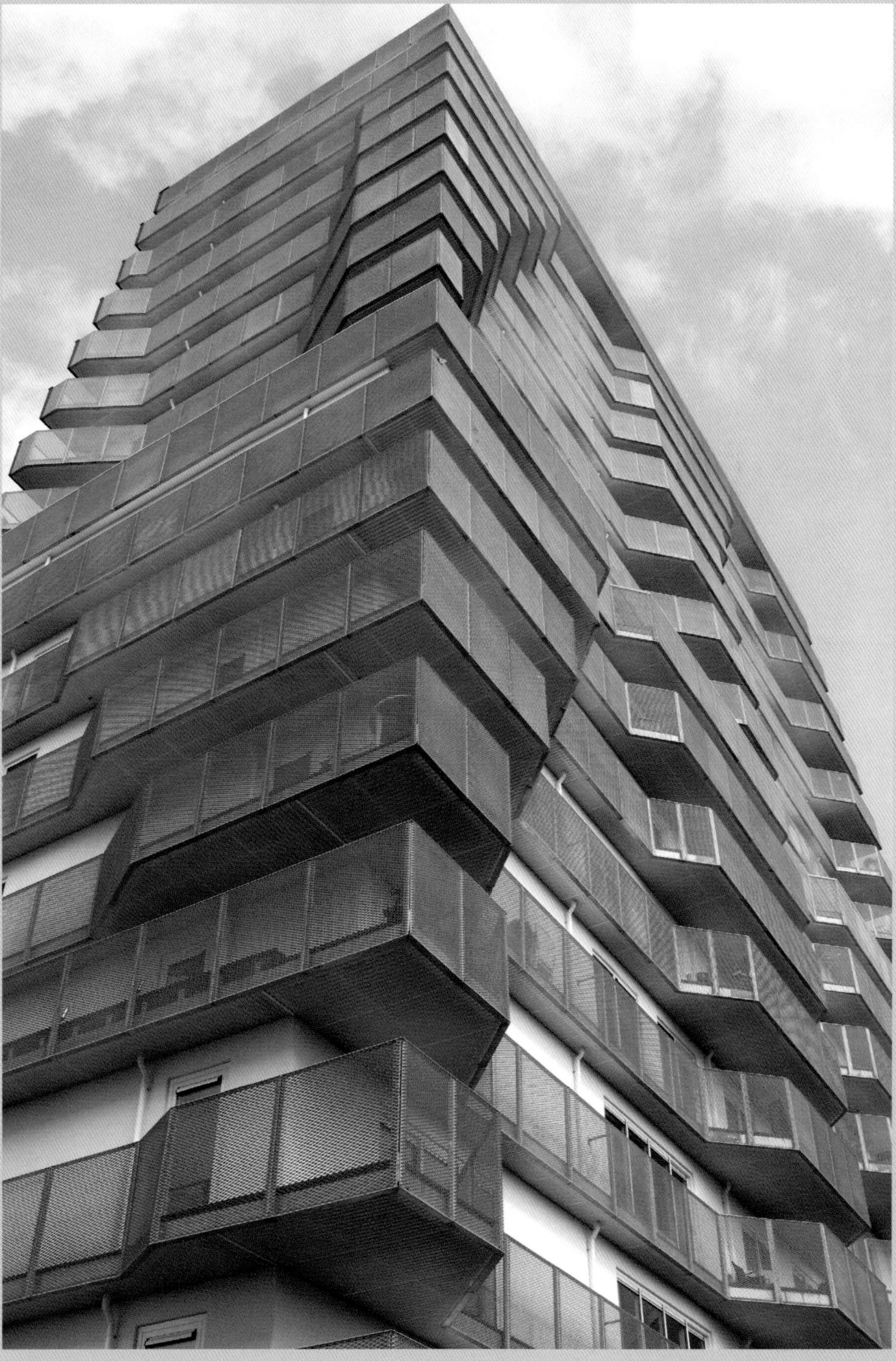

The architect needs an idea to help make the conflicting questions and requirements of the brief understandable and answerable.

For example: 'This cinema will be about the contrast between light and dark' – this is a concept. It can help the architect to make decisions that are consistent and meaningful, however idiosyncratic, in the context of so many variables and possibilities. Continuing the example: 'People enter the black box of the auditorium and bask in the glow of the projection. The narrative of the film will lead them to experience emotions ranging from light to dark. Therefore, the design of the position and form of the windows in the foyer will be significant to the occupants and the materials chosen for that space will be dualistic and strongly contrasting.'

Over the course of a project, an architect will develop a concept that can be used to make choices about everything from construction materials to the emotional experience of the building users. It can unite several competing demands into an overall idea to prevent the building becoming a cacophony of disparate elements.

However, a concept can be far more than a creative problem-solving device. It can be the story that the architect tells to provoke images in their own mind as well as the minds of tutors, clients and collaborators. This enables a closer mutual understanding while the proposal is being developed. Crucially, a strong concept is one that will resonate with everyone who uses the building because it has translated from idea to meaning. This meaning should communicate to the building's occupants on many levels and elevate their experience of using it over a long period of time.

Earlier in the chapter, we discussed the predictive optimism, enhanced perception, empirical invention and craft of the architect. These qualities compel the architect to inject an idea, and therefore meaning, into their architecture. They cannot solve complex architectural problems without first asking, 'What is the problem?' The search for meaning within our surroundings is a central human concern. This is why we are all fascinated by, and can engage with, architecture. The discipline constantly escapes attempts to define it in absolute terms. It is in these gaps between answers, and in the refusal of architects to be pigeon-holed, that the strength of architectural design can be found.

Triggers for architectural activity

Some architects choose to portray design either as the product of a gradual, rational and methodical series of moves or as a sudden moment of inspiration. Most architects would describe a mixture of both but value either inspiration or method more than the other. The variation in the perception of design activity would seem to stem from the fact that some architects believe the moment of design is provoked by activity and some by reflection.

Whatever their position along this continuum, most architects would recognise the following description: the process of architectural design is a creative act that requires the designer to employ their full range of skills, which takes time and requires periods of activity and of reflection. This balanced approach is needed to solve architectural problems and manage their complexity.

The debate about how and when design happens is symptomatic of the fact that there is no single accepted design process for architects to follow. Just as the complexity of the design task must be broken down and understood internally in the mind of the individual, each architect must also make their own decisions about how to proceed with the task. This becomes part of the architect's developing design process. Every architect follows their own design process, which has been informed by their education and experience, and which adapts to respond to the different kinds of design problems that they encounter.

[An architectural concept] 'should be something that overrides all scales. An architectural concept would need to be so clear that it runs through all scales and once that's communicated and understood, any problem on site, at any scale, should be able to be solved.'
Judith Lösing, East

NL Architects: Prisma housing › **Developing a concept** › Klein Dytham architecture: Billboard Building

Klein Dytham architecture: Billboard Building

Name: Billboard Building
Completed: 2005
Location: Tokyo, Japan
Programme: Shop
Height: Two floors

Billboard Building viewed at its narrowest point

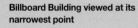

The design process

Klein Dytham architecture was founded in Tokyo in 1991 by Astrid Klein and Mark Dytham. Their multi-disciplinary practice encompasses architecture, interiors, public spaces and installations. They also lecture and teach internationally. This case study illustrates their approach to developing an architectural concept and applying it to both develop a design and communicate it to the building's client and users.

The project

Klein Dytham architecture work in a rapidly changing city with an appetite for stylistic innovation and few aesthetic restrictions. Their response to this demanding environment is to create architecture that is memorable through the ideas it communicates: the building may be short-lived but people will remember fondly the positive message that it projected. This approach requires the creation of inventive and engaging architectural concepts that convey a clear message about what and who the building is for.

In their book *Klein Dytham architecture – Tokyo calling*, Astrid Klein explains that 'We don't want to be elitist and our approach is far from academic. Architecture is all about the visual; you never find a note inside that describes the concept. Just look at it. See it.'

The Billboard Building demonstrates very clearly how architects can make creative use of an architectural concept. Every architect will give you a different answer to the question 'what is an architectural concept?', but in essence, a concept is the idea behind a project that elevates the building from just being a building towards being architecture. This idea should be understandable not just to the architect but to the people who walk past and who use the building.

Developing a concept > Klein Dytham architecture: Billboard Building > Finding a process

Interior of Billboard Building

Located on a tiny site tapering from 2.5m to 0.6m wide in a prominent position, these challenges became virtues. Klein Dytham architecture recognised that the slender building would be almost entirely façade and that this was a condition similar to the billboards nearby. Their concept was therefore to design a building that would in effect become an occupied façade and their treatment of this would ensure that the shop would advertise itself as effectively as a billboard. One of the most striking qualities of this building is the legibility and resolution of its concept.

Astrid Klein and Mark Dytham have also devised 'PechaKucha Night', which is another way to learn about architecture and the way that architects think (Pecha Kucha is Japanese for the sound of conversation). It is an informal event where a group of designers, in front of an audience, are asked to talk about 20 images, each shown for 20 seconds (see www.pecha-kucha.org). This is a simple way for designers to show their work and reveal the conceptual ideas behind it. Connections can be made between different strands of thought from other designers, encouraging a more dynamic and reflective discussion of ideas than would occur at a conventional lecture or crit.

The design project

Shop as illuminated billboard

Photographer: Daici Ano

'Being nearly all front, we let it be what it so obviously wanted to be – an inhabitable billboard.'

Klein Dytham architecture

1

2

Horst Rittel's diagram of four 'design processes for generating variety and reducing variety':

1 Linear sequence

2 Testing or scanning

3 Systematic production of alternatives

4 Forming alternatives in a multi-step process

Analysing the process of design

In his book *Tools for Ideas: Introduction to Architectural Design*, Christian Gänshirt shows four alternative diagrams that Horst Rittel used to describe the design process. The first and simplest diagram, a 'linear sequence', shows activity followed by a decision, which leads to further activity, which leads in turn to another decision and so on. In theory, this linear process could describe a very experienced architect who is solving a problem similar to previous, successfully solved ones. However, when applied to architectural problems, this makes the assumption that an architect would wish to solve a similar problem in a similar way rather than to continually seek innovation, as most would strive to do.

The second diagram, 'testing and scanning', shows an attempt by the designer to use the first solution that occurs to them. When this does not produce the desired result, the designer returns to the beginning and tries a different solution. The third diagram, 'systematic production of alternatives', shows a designer who is consciously setting up several alternative approaches and exploring them before using critical judgement to make a decision. The fourth diagram, 'forming alternatives in a multi-step process', describes a designer who will develop multiple solutions but with self-imposed constraints to reduce the number of alternatives to a manageable amount.

The fourth version seems the closest to the reality of the design process. It admits the imposition of constraints by the designer in order to make the task manageable and therefore introduces an element of arbitrariness and subjectivity, which certainly exists, however logical the reasons for the decision made by the designer.

3   4

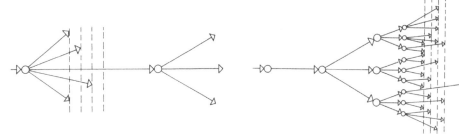

This diagrammatic approach is useful for defining and reflecting upon the differences between the approaches of individual architects; or at least, their perceived approaches. However, it is impossible to use such diagrams to provide a definitive record of the actual process followed. In any given project, design decision-making is too rapid, complex and messy to be so neatly defined or recorded.

Understanding the process of design

There are other ways beyond diagrams to describe the process of design but these also have their own limitations. More experiential descriptions include monographs, case studies, theoretical works, architectural biographies and interviews. These provide an insight into an individual's perception of their own process or that of the architect being studied. It should be remembered that these accounts are retrospective, subjective and, often by necessity, partial.

Despite the limitations of trying to define individual design processes there is a value in only being able to report a retrospective and partial version of events; we need any account of a process to remain general. If the description is too precise, it cannot be comprehended in a usable way and reapplied elsewhere in an adapted form.

SHoP Architects PC: 290 Mulberry

Name: 290 Mulberry
Completed: 2009
Client: Cardinal Investments
Location: New York, USA
Programme: Nine
residences, commercial
space located at ground
floor and cellar
Height: 13 floors including
penthouse
Gross floor area: 2,490m²

SHoP Architects PC was founded in New York in 1996 by Kimberly J Holden, Gregg A Pasquarelli, Christopher R Sharples, Coren D Sharples and William W Sharples. Their backgrounds encompass architecture, fine arts, structural engineering, finance and business management. They teach, lecture, publish and exhibit their work internationally. This case study illustrates how design thinking and digital tools were used to resolve the complex form and construction of a residential and commercial building.

The project

SHoP Architects' approach to architectural design is to consider the project within several different contexts simultaneously: design, finance and technology. They are known for their use of emerging computer-aided design and manufacturing technology to create innovative designs and to re-connect the design process to the construction process. By using technology to process complex design data and construct innovative forms directly from that data, SHoP Architects can produce bespoke forms more efficiently and more fluently than would otherwise be possible.

North-west corner under construction

The variations in the undulating brick façade are all composed from a single repeated panel mould.

290 Mulberry is a residential building located in the NoLita district of New York. It is adjacent to the Puck Building, a distinctively decorative, historic masonry building. The form and materiality of the building responds directly to strict local zoning and building code regulations. These limit the enclosure to projection over the property line by ten per cent intervals for every 9.3 square metres. This was reinterpreted by SHoP Architects as an opportunity to design an undulating skin for the building.

The design focused on creating a single undulating panel that could be used repeatedly in different configurations on corners, around windows, and at the base and top, and yet still give a lively and varied form to the façade. Non-load-bearing brickwork allowed SHoP Architects to stagger the projection of individual bricks within the panel, giving further texture and variation at a more detailed scale. All this richness had to be achieved within the tight restrictions of the building codes as well as the structural and constructional limitations of the materials.

The design process

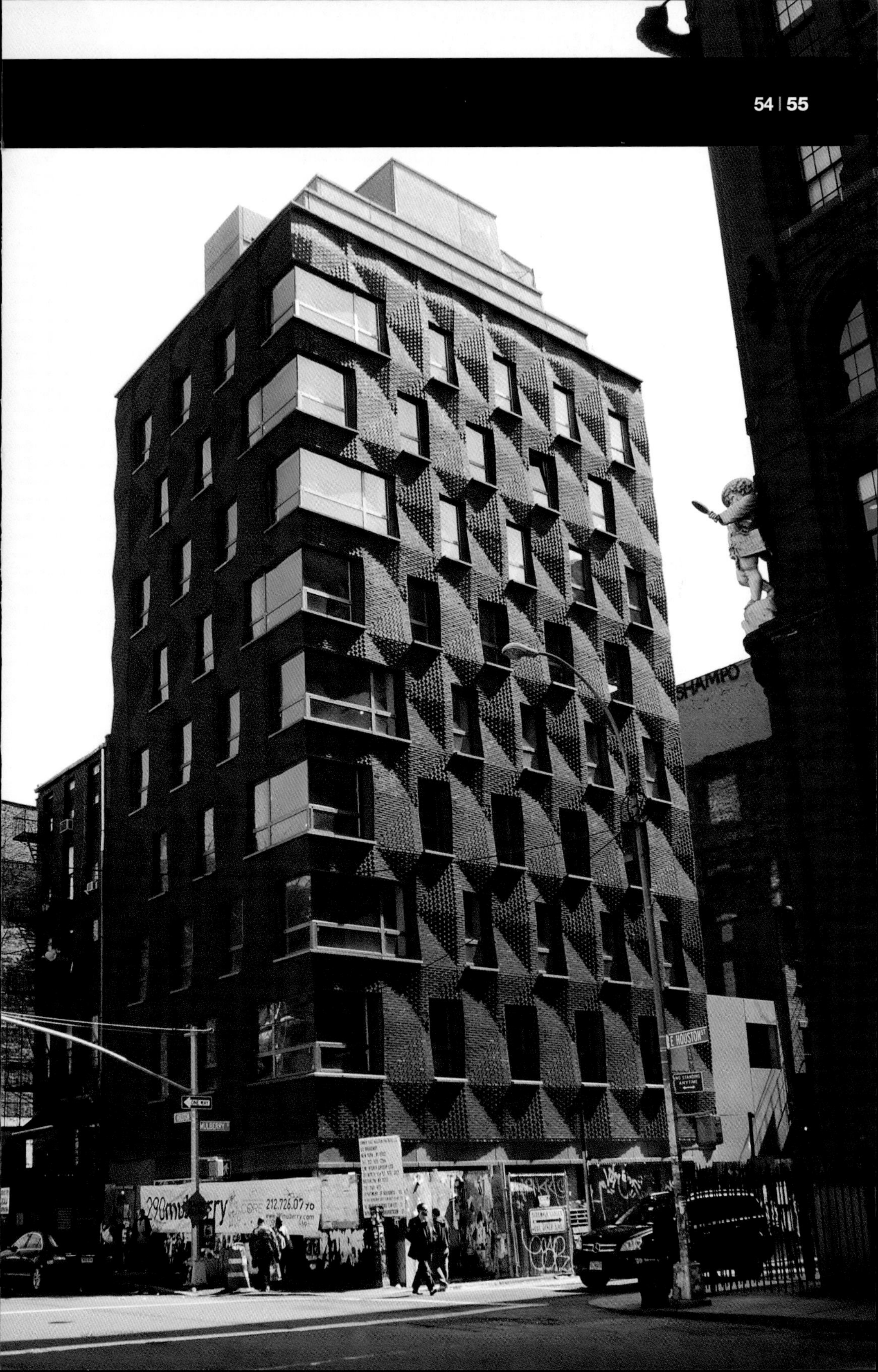
SHAMPO
E HOUSTON ST
ONE WAY
MULBERRY

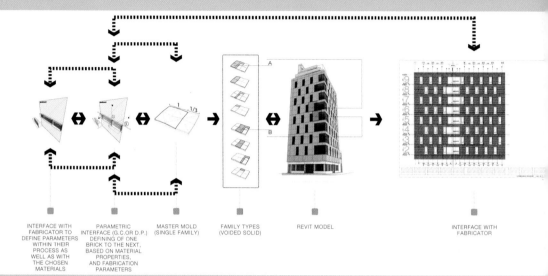

| INTERFACE WITH FABRICATOR TO DEFINE PARAMETERS WITHIN THEIR PROCESS AS WELL AS WITH THE CHOSEN MATERIALS | PARAMETRIC INTERFACE (G.C.OR D.P.) DEFINING OF ONE BRICK TO THE NEXT, BASED ON MATERIAL PROPERTIES, AND FABRICATION PARAMETERS | MASTER MOLD (SINGLE FAMILY) | FAMILY TYPES (VOIDED SOLID) | REVIT MODEL | INTERFACE WITH FABRICATOR |

above:
Façade development

Diagram showing the process of façade development: the limits set by the fabricator; the limits of brick projections; the master panel mould; the variations possible within one master mould; a three-dimensional 'building information modelling'; and the fabrication drawings used to make the panels.

right:
Parametric development

Screen shot showing parametric development of the undulating panel design. The panels were designed and drawn using software that tracks design changes in real time, increasing the efficiency and reducing the risk of errors in a project.

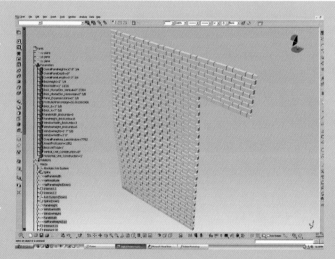

Creation of panel mould on CNC milling machine

A flexible plastic form liner was produced from an original positive Computer Numerical Control (CNC) milled from digital drawings.

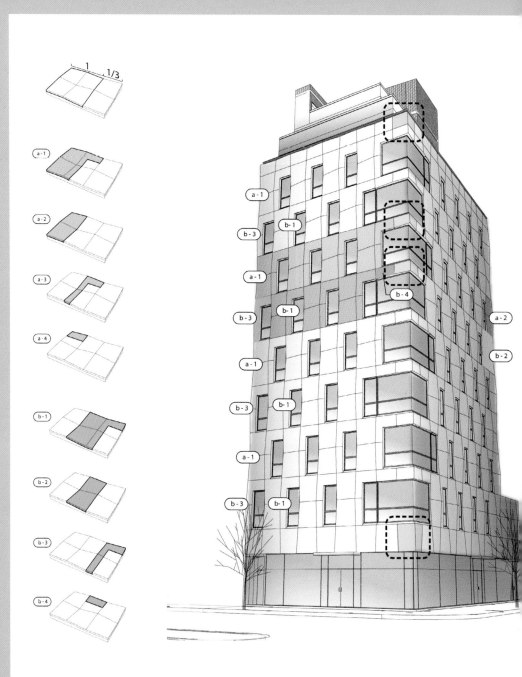

Software such as 'Digital Project' and 'Generative Components' were used to help model and resolve the complex geometry as the design evolved, and to ensure that the limits on proportional projection over the property line were not exceeded. In addition, the panels were designed and drawn using software that fed the data into a Building Information Modelling (BIM) program called 'Revit'. BIM tracks design changes in real time, increasing the efficiency, incorporating engineering data, calculating the changing costs and reducing the risk of errors in a complex project.

Data from the drawing process was also used to assist with the construction of the undulating form that had been designed. A flexible plastic form liner was produced from an original positive Computer Numerical Control (CNC), milled from digital drawings produced by SHoP Architects and a fabricator. This liner needed to be very accurate to ensure the correct placement of bricks and mortar joints. It was used to hold the bricks in place within the form while being cast. The resulting precast panels were transported to site ready for installation.

The use of digital tools to process data produced by the architects' drawings in real time is not only efficient, it also allows the designer to take on more complex design problems without compromising the ambition for the project. The consequences of different design options can be more quickly and more fully understood before the designer has become irrevocably committed to them. This form of predictive modelling gives the architect both visual imagery and interpreted data; with this, they can make a critical judgement that is simultaneously objective and subjective about how to proceed with their design.

Three-dimensional computer model

This model was used to show the location of the differently configured undulating panels on the façade.

'Make the office a lab, a boardroom, a theatre, a classroom.'
SHoP Architects PC

In many ways architecture is a very human and responsive medium. Architects seek to contribute to the solution of a perceived problem or need. Great skill and care are required to accurately perceive or predict these needs. When built projects get this wrong they often do so in a spectacular way, with high social, environmental, political and financial costs. Although architecture is responsive, it is not passive. Architects do not wait to be asked to solve these problems; they seek them out and strive for innovation.

Creative cycle: attitudes and actions

There are different attitudes and activities that an architect must adopt in order to follow an innovative and creative process of design. The cycle from one stage to the next is not continuous. The architect may even skip some stages or move back and forth between them.

Complexity: this inspires or provokes the response that will improve the designer's understanding of an architectural problem.

Challenge: the architect must either question the status quo or redefine the problem in order to understand it and make an innovative proposal.

Creativity: the architect must be open to new ideas. At times, this can be a playful and serendipitous experience. At others, the letting-go of previous knowledge or presumptions can be uncomfortable and difficult: it is essentially a deliberate loss of control.

Confidence: it is important to retain confidence that the process will lead to a proposal. The architect needs to be ready to make mistakes during the design process. It helps to remember that decisions made during the design process only really exist on paper and that it is possible to explore an alternative option later. A good designer will find another solution if their previous one has been demonstrated as unworkable. A good idea is never really wasted. It will either be adaptable or useful for another project.

Communication: once a proposal has begun to form, its meaning and idea must be communicated so that others can understand it and the architect can reflect upon it. Architectural communication is usually in the form of drawings, models or words. Communication is the first step in helping a proposal to become real.

Critical judgement: this is constantly used for decision making and to develop an idea.

Control: once a proposal has been adopted, control helps to refine and execute the idea. It is important to control the idea (have good reason to believe that it is relevant, to communicate it and also make it real) so that users of the built work will also share in its meaning.

The design project is common to both architectural education and practice. It is not only the means by which buildings are built, it is also a vehicle for solving problems, experimentation, improving skills and communication of new ideas. It is important to remember that neither the process of design nor the course of a design project follow a neatly linear course. One project may start with client, another with site. Design might progress to a particular stage and then return to another, or even miss out a stage. Certain parts of a design might be at the beginning while others are already advanced.

This chapter of the book divides the design project into five, roughly chronological parts, starting with the client and ending with their occupation of the finished project. In accordance with the non-linear nature of design, this chapter can be read in at least two different ways. It can be read by architect: interviews and examples of work from five architects enables a comparison of their distinct approaches to design. It can also be read by stage: each section provides information and advice on typical activities undertaken in that stage of the design project.

Each of the five parts examines student design diaries, which help describe their parallel experience. There are exercises to try, which demonstrate methods that could be used to develop a design project at this stage. Where possible, connections have been made between design studio activity in practice and education. In addition to practising and teaching, the five architects interviewed have written and lectured on their work. Reference to their books can be found in Further Resources on page 172.

Project: Young Vic Theatre
Location: London, UK
Architect: Haworth Tompkins
Date: 2006

Night-time view of renovated theatre auditorium, showing the relationship between the site context and the materials chosen by the architects.

**Typical activities
at this stage**
Client meetings
Sketching
Recording ideas
Organisational diagrams
Gathering information
Opening up possibilities
Managing complexity
Research
Collaboration
Feedback
Setting priorities

**Project: Tufnell Park School
Location: Islington, London, UK
Architect: East
Date: 2006**

Internal perspective montage.

**Most student projects do not have a real client involved
with the project, although real project briefs are often
adapted and imaginary clients may be included. Tutors
and visiting critics partly form the role of proxy-client and
the project brief will be developed by research into the
given client.**

Most live projects emerge in order to fulfil the need of a
client. This need forms the basis of the project brief. A client
may decide that they need to build a new shop, contact an
architect and commission them to design and manage the
project. However there are many variations to this scenario.
The client may be a developer who needs to make a profit on
the development and therefore is not the intended user of the
building. The architect may be designing for people whom
they are not able to meet or consult. The client, the user and
their various needs and constraints, must be identified and
understood by the architect.

The brief normally has complexities that are not immediately
apparent. The brief is not a static document handed to
the architect at the beginning of the project; it must be
developed in collaboration with the client and users an often
has to evolve to cope with changes in circumstances as the
project develops. The direction, ambition and nature of the
project can be radically altered by the interpretation of the
brief that is agreed by the architect and client. The architect
is normally the driver for the detailed development of the brief
and the process of discovery that this uncovers. They must
seek to answer needs and aspirations that are both mundane
and poetic.

'We always try to locate the need for architecture and that is very much about influencing the brief.'

Dan Jessen, East

lights

mirror

chestnut tree

kitchen storage

wet play area

disabled toilet

sheltered playdeck

tall timber skirting bo

East

East is an architecture, landscape and urban design practice based in London. Its three directors are Julian Lewis, Dann Jessen and Judith Lösing. They are interested in places, their uses and the way they come about; cities, spaces within them, buildings and landscapes. Their work is recognised for its innovative role in adjusting and improving urban fabric and its uses. Their experience in considering the broad range of people who will use their urban landscape interventions informs an engagement with all who will use their architecture. This engagement begins during the development of the brief and continues during fund-raising and construction of the project through to occupation of the building. Their work ranges from large-scale landscape and urban planning projects to community buildings and interventions to improve public space. They are particularly interested in the potential of previously disregarded edge places to become sites of generosity where public space can be formed to meet the needs of local people. The directors of East are design advisors at the London Development Agency and they teach at London Metropolitan University and the Accademia di Mendrisio in Switzerland, as well as lecturing internationally.

With great skill, East has used the opportunities afforded by its complex public realm projects to explore creative means of connecting with the many and varied users of its public spaces. The practice has translated this knowledge into methods for developing effective briefs with other complex client bodies, such as schools and community centres. Its involvement in large-scale landscape and urban projects also links to its work in formulating strategic plans and design guides, such as the Transport for London Streetscape Guidance, which is another form of brief writing.

Interview with Julian Lewis, Dann Jessen and Judith Lösing of East

When you formulated the Transport for London Streetscape Guidance, what ambitions did you set for yourselves and the brief?

Dann Jessen

It's important to understand that the client is London and that therefore you don't rely on the express aspirations of the paying client only, but look at the need for the work that you are doing and raise the aspirations for it yourself. That project was special because it stretched across London. Normally we would be really interested in the specifics of a local situation; with the Streetscape Guidance we needed to understand the spatial and cultural characteristics of large chunks of the city.

Judith Lösing

Transport for London's ambition is not necessarily about making a decent background for ordinary life to happen. Their impetus is about making safe crossings, following guidelines. Our role was always to bring it back to what it is like spatially and how it can be simplified.

Does your application of the term 'client' beyond the person paying for the project change your approach to an architectural problem?

Dann Jessen

With public realm clients the paying client is not necessarily the one who's going to use the project, who has most ambitions for it, who will live with it. Because we have the mindset that the client group can be big and multi-headed and ambitious, that means that we are not afraid of looking outside the red line site boundary. It's in our mindset that people outside the red line are also part of the client group and that influences what we can do inside the red line. If you can actually push up against the boundary and think beyond that, then that influences the centre.

Clients, users and brief › Site, context and place

WATERFRONT LEISURE CENTRE
SUCCESSFUL IN TERMS OF USE.
THE ONLY BUILDING WITH A
FRONTAGE THAT SAYS 'WOOLWICH
IS FOR YOU'.
NOT GOOD RELATIONSHIP WITH RIVER
COULD BE EXPANDED/ADDED TO.

TEAGARDEN
THE CONCEPT OF A TEAGARDEN LIMITS
THE POTENTIAL FOR THIS SPACE. IT
SHOULD BE MORE OPEN, MORE
PERMEABLE. THE LEISURE MIX COULD
BE GOOD IF IT CAN BE MADE TO WORK,
BUT THE LAYOUT OF TOWN, LINK BUILDINGS
WITH VIEWS & WAYS BETWEEN VENUS
ENABLE A MUCH LARGER SPACE
TO BE PROVIDED. A BEACH LIKE
SPACE ANIMATED WITH USES
FROM BERESFORD SQUARE RIGHT
DOWN TO THE RIVER.

RIVERFRONT
HISTORICALLY THE RIVERFRONT DID NOT
EXIST. TODAY THE SPACES AT THE RIVER EDGES
ARE BEING UNLOCKED, AND PRISED OPEN UNDER MAR-
PRESSURE. UNFORTUNATELY HOUSES + RIVERWALKS +
GREEN PARK ARE NOT ENOUGH TO A VIBRANT PL
TO USE ALL DAY, AT WEEKENDS AND IN THE EVENINGS
USES. MORE SPACE, MORE PERMEABILITY + MORE
BUILDINGS ARE NEEDED. TOWN PERMALT WIDER RIVER V
WALKWAYS, ADD PIERS ETC. SIGNAGE FROM RIVER?

WOOLWICH FERRY
PART OF THE IDENTITY OF THE
PLACE. WHEN/IF IT GOES, IT
COULD BECOME A PEDESTRIAN
FERRY; INCLUDE NORTH WOOLWICH
IN WOOLWICH. KEEP KIND OF THIS
SECTION OF RIVER. USE IT TO
SEE WOOLWICH FROM THE RIVER.
INCLUDE IT IN RIVER BUS ROUTES.
NEED TO SPEAK TO PLA +
ENVIRONMENT AGENCY

WATERFRONT TRANSIT
OPTIONS FOR ROUTES IN
DISCUSSION. WE NEED TO
TEST THESE, (ALONG WITH
TFL + COUNCIL REQUIREMENTS)
ALONGSIDE OPPORTUNITIES
ARISING FROM FRAMEWORK

ROAD
- OPTIONS NEED
- DOWNGRADE,
- SEMI-TUNNEL
- DIVERSION UP IN

CROSSRAIL
WE NEED TO SHOW WHAT THIS
COULD MEAN/BRING FOR
POSITIVE RESULT

MAST POND WHARF/AREA
PART OF THE NEW RIVERFRONT. WE
NEED TO RECEIVE INFO. ON PLANNING
APPLICATION

MACBEAN
- GOOD PLACE FOR
ARTRAIL. GOOD ROUTES,
GOOD RELATIONSHIP WITH
'TEAGARDEN'. DENSE MIX
ALL NEEDED, WITH
SUPPRESSED ROAD
RUNNING THROUGH.

VIEW IMPORTANT
SAY EM.

ST. MARYS CHURCH
- MCP BID. LIGHTING,
HISTORICALLY SIGNIFICANT,
IMPROVE ACCESS,
PRESENCE

BUS/DEBENHAMS
- GOOD POSSIBILITIES
FOR KEEPING
PARKING OFF
GROUND LEVEL
WOULD BE GOOD
TO TEST

HOUSING

PEGGY MIDDLETON
- SCENARIOS NEED TO BE
MADE TO INDICATE HOW
TO DEVELOP IT TO:
- MAKE STRATEGIC CONNECTIONS
TO THE SOUTH WEST
- MIX EMPLOYMENT, RESIDENTIAL,
COMMUNITY, PUBLIC SPACE.

ISLAND
- WE NEED TO
RECEIVE INFO.
POTENTIAL FOR
EXCITING MIX.
MUST NOT BE
MEDIOCRE

CAR PARK
- WHEN SAINSBURYS
MOVE, A CHANCE TO
REINCORPORATE GROUND
FLOOR AS POSITIVE PART OF
PUBLIC REALM BECOMES
POSSIBLE.

MILITARY
- THEY DON'T NEED ALL
THAT LAND (?)

GLA
- BT TOO EXPENSIVE TO MOVE
- LOOK AT HOW TO MOVE
AROUND/ACROSS RAILWAY
HOW TO BE MORE AMBITIOUS
IN TERMS OF DENSITY, USE, PRESENCE,
LINKAGE ACROSS RAILWAY, EXTENSION
OF POWIS ST. HOUSING WITH PARK AS
BRIDGE

ARSENAL
- LOOK AT + TEST POSSIBILITI
ROUTES, SPACES, MORE &
MIXED USES, RELATIONSH
'TEARAY' (VISUALLY)
STRENGTHENIN
BUILDING (10) OPTIONS FOR

HOUSING
THERE IS A VAST
SWATHE OF HOUSING SURROUNDING
THE TOWN CENTRE. SOME AREAS
WORK WELL, MANY DO NOT. QUALITY
OF STOCK + SPACES IS POOR. THERE
IS A NEED TO: INCREASE MIX +
DIVERSITY OF MIX OF TENURE, OF
TYPES OF HOUSING, OF CHOICE. INCREASE
QUALITY OF BUILDINGS + SPACES,
PROVIDE SERVICES TO SUPPORT EXISTING
+ NEW COMMUNITIES (HEALTH ETC.)
IMPROVE LINKS TO TOWN CENTRE.
THE HOUSING SHOULD BECOME PART OF
THE TOWN.
INCREASING DENSITY IS ESSENTIAL, TO
MEET NEED FOR GROWTH, PAY FOR
IMPROVEMENTS TO EXISTING, RESTRUCTURE
PHYSICAL ARRANGEMENTS, ALLOW PROPE
MIX AND INCREASE PERCEPTION OF THI
AREA AS A DESIRABLE PLACE TO LIVE.

MORE TILES TO C
AREAS ARE NEEDED

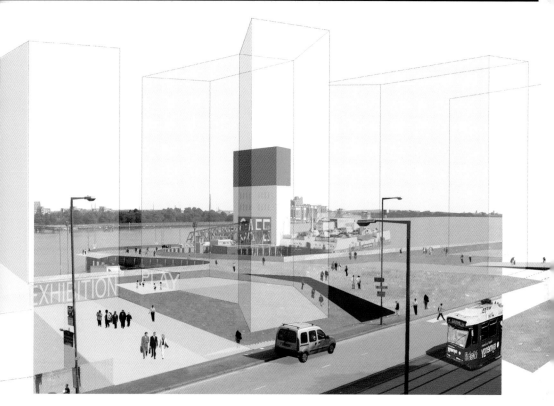

Project: Woolwich Development Framework
Location: London, UK
Architect: East
Date: 2003

left:
Development framework study.
East has developed a technique
called 'hairy drawing'. It involves
several people sitting around a table
drawing, talking and making notes
on the same piece of paper, to record
everything they know about a
project. It helps the group to
remember what is important; to
communicate this to the others and
help each other to solve the design
problem at hand.

above:
This strategy and planning
framework drawing shows what
might be but does not dictate the
architectural solution.

Clients, users and brief › Site, context and place

When you are developing the brief with clients would you call it collaboration, consultation, negotiation?

Judith Lösing

We use 'consultation' but it feels as if: 'we've designed something and are you happy with that?' which is not how we want to work. Collaboration doesn't feel quite right because that implies that clients and users have an equal role to us and in the end we want to keep hold of the design. So maybe it is a 'negotiation'. We are setting ourselves in the position to understand everybody's agenda and then we bring forward proposals that hopefully can be negotiated between a number of different parties. 'Involvement' is nice, it feels more active and propositional.

Dann Jessen

Some architects are OK with presenting different options and then roughly go with the consensus. We tend to find that there aren't that many good options so we would rather try to work with people and enable them to have a conversation about materials or colour or texture.

Judith Lösing

There's also distrust about the consensus that tends to happen on one day where people put up Post-It notes or if one person brings lots of their friends. It's very important that we feel that the proposition is right and that we are creating a meaningful discussion.

Dann Jessen

There's always a skills transfer thing going on in the beginning, because people are not necessarily educated to be able to discuss the design. What really impresses me is how a few hours into a workshop a resident will suddenly start talking about the importance of the texture of the brick, because she will have thought about that forever and enjoyed it forever. She will just never actually have expressed this, have had the words or somebody listening to it. It is impressive how many observations you can get out of people very quickly by valuing the situation that you are in.

Judith Lösing

Sussex Road School was a very good example of where a special client relationship was built up very early. The client team is not duplicating the role of the designer but they are being educated to be clients. The children were playing out the problems that the school had, so they were playing the deputy head teacher who didn't have a private toilet with a mirror to put on her make-up. We tried to steer it away from the children saying 'we want a green sofa'. It's more about them being aware of the issues and giving us a very detailed brief that we couldn't come up with because we haven't been using the school to the same extent that the students and their parents have done for years. In a series of further meetings we then told them what we understood the issues were and tested if that was right. Sometimes we are making our models together and other times bringing in models that can be manipulated.

Dann Jessen

Models are much easier to enter into than drawings because there's a very direct relationship between them and the spatial reality. It's amazing how much imagination people have, though. Sometimes their input can be so rich in ideas that can go straight in to a project, whereas at other times of course, it might be a bit more like establishing a common ground or understanding.

Judith Lösing

There's a moment where we come up with a concept that we think answers all of the problems that are there. At that stage we try to describe that concept and make the clients enthusiastic about the leap we have taken. This can be adjusted if necessary.

Dann Jessen

What we find is that people are worried about change and then it becomes really important to articulate what is good about the place as it is, both in physical terms and also culturally or in terms of social relationships. There is a kind of economy of means built into the whole idea of valuing places as they are and adjusting them to make the most of the opportunities that exist.

Clients, users and brief › Site, context and place

Do you draw while you are talking to clients?

Dann Jessen
Yes, it's very useful to not be afraid of doing that. To have a relationship between what's being said and what it could mean. We use annotations on drawings because the combination of the drawing and text is able to communicate very efficiently – even in spatial drawings or photo montages.

Judith Lösing
I think one is drawing with the client to make them party to the development of the design. With their words on it they can feel a different sense of ownership, but I think it's also something we do between us [in the office].

Dann Jessen
We spend a lot of time observing places and we talk to people. These conversations are often captured in drawings. So every time we have had a meeting we might draw rather than write minutes. We draw minutes on a plan so that the outcome is spatial and able to directly inform proposals for adjustments to the place.

Judith Lösing
These early consultations tend to be part of the brief that comes with public-sector clients. Often they can be made very useful. They're not just about 'tell us about what you think' or 'what's wrong here?' We try to make them an early one-to-one testing of what the place could be. For example, in Kender Gardens we made a large sandpit in the shape of the park as a model for a consultation day. We wanted to show our proposals but also see if children would like to play with sand, which we proposed as an alternative to rubber safety surfaces.

Dann Jessen
If you actually map all of the stuff that makes a place then that becomes your client; the place gets a presence and it becomes about adjusting and adding to this, rather than just wishing for a blank canvas.

Julian Lewis
The mapping is actually quite creative. It's not just documenting, it's selecting things which we believe have value and working with those different extents, different materials, different cultural layers.

Project: Hastings Nursery
Location: Hastings and St Leonards, UK
Architect: East
Date: 2008

The play area was designed in consultation with the children who would use it. The architects' observations of the children at play are evident in their drawings and inform their proposals for the new play space.

The design project

**Project: Rainham Riverside
Walkway and Cafe
Location: London, UK
Architect: East
Date: Ongoing**

This project forms part of the East
London Green Grid Framework.
At the site, Rainham Marshes, an
industrial estate meets the River
Thames. The site is typical of many
of East's projects, being on the
edge of several different conditions.
In order to tie these together and
increase the use of the place,
a series of adjustments are made
to the river walk to provide views
and connections with the low-lying
area beyond the river. East's cafe
provides a meeting place; its golden
cladding evokes the Three Crowns,
a demolished pub previously
occupying the site.

Many of your drawings have a narrative quality.

Dann Jessen

I think that's got to do with our interest in public situations.
The drawings need to be able to tell a story and engage
with the situation in terms of spaces and use, but also
in terms of the culture of the place. Plans, sections and
elevations are really for the production of buildings and for
pinning things down.

**Can we talk about your 'hairy drawing' technique – this
idea of drawing out as much as you possibly can until
there's no more? Do you use this to understand the full
complexity of a situation?**

Julian Lewis

[Rainham Riverside] has come out of the process of hairy
drawing, amongst other things, and that's the only reason
why this project includes the river and the industrial buildings
and the river walk.

Dann Jessen
I found with Rainham Riverside that the client sometimes
wished us to remove proposals from our drawing because
they thought they were outside their sphere of influence.
Some of these things are now happening completely
independently of the original client.

Judith Lösing
A brief for the public has to be ambitious: there are so many
layers of ownership needs and different opportunities, so it
can't be straightforward.

Julian Lewis
I think the technique to do with complexity is not to meet
complexity with complex solutions because it then ends
up in a mess. You've got to have clear thinking; simple
conceptual approaches.

Dann Jessen
Yes. Clarity and communication are not about reduction but
actually about generosity, I think.

Interview summary

Although most clients will provide a brief at the beginning of a project, East's work is testament to the need for the architect to question and challenge its fundamental aims, nature and scope: does the given brief fail to take advantage of any opportunities or needs? In addition, the identity of the actual client must be interrogated: are there any clients or users who have a stake in the project and who should be included in the design process? With so many projects lacking a definable client, East takes the view that the place itself is the client and that its needs should be recognised and met. This approach is valuable for students tackling a studio-design project without an easily definable client.

As the interview with East shows, this questioning must be intelligent and productive if it is to succeed, rather than unsettle or undermine the client. The architect should bring creativity to any situation where information is to be gleaned from clients, to ensure that the quality of thought and aspiration for the project remains high. East's working methods ensure that clients are given the opportunity to learn how to be clients: how the design process works and what their role is within it. It is important the architect remains in control of his or her own design process and retains clarity about the authorship of the work. The architect's skills in drawn, verbal and written communication are key to success.

The benefits of learning to ask the right questions in a creative way are that the extent and richness of a complex design problem can be discovered and managed as part of the design process.

Project: Sussex Road School
Location: Tonbridge, Kent, UK
Architect: East
Date: 2009

right: Sketch model showing the concept of a decorated façade. This later developed into a timber cladding that was branded with the school symbols of honey bees, acorns and oak leaves.

far right: The process of involving pupils with the changes at their school began during the brief development. This was continued during the construction phase when pupils were invited to brand the timber cladding.

below right: This brief was developed as the result of a consultation workshop with pupils at Sussex Road School. Role play was used to identify the issues and activities to be addressed by the design and the activities that the design should encourage. See the description of the workshop on page 71.

'When all opportunities are still open and when we are allowed to look at places and leap ahead in terms of imagination and possibilities: I think that's a very exciting moment. It is, however, also very exciting when that is being crushed up against by the reality of the client.'
Dann Jessen, East

Sussex Road School: the teacher and pupils' brief for the architect

Pragmatic

Welcoming space

Display areas

Friendly reception

More private loos

Extra toilet for visitors

Elegant room for Mr A

Huge windows and wide views

Cups of tea

Better organised photocopy room

Space reflecting the vibrancy of the school

More space for Mrs F and Mrs D

Remove clutter

Effective storage systems

Clear signs

Soft furniture

Plants

Mrs F and Mrs D facing visitors

Child-friendly storage in Joy's room

Mosaic

Lots of fish

More children's work for adults to see at the entrance

More room and desk space in the office

Wishlist

Yellow brick road

Coloured glass

Soothing music

Double-storey entrance

Mr A on top

Extra room

Bubbles

Visitor room

Space for community

Buggy shed

Delivery storage

Fish and plastic fish

Baby massage

Living room

Sleepovers

Kiosk to sell apples

A transparent corridor

Curvy path or fence

Mr A going down the waterslide

Electronic back massage

Bubbly lifts and elevators

Intercom systems

Multi-sensory rooms

Baby slide

Lights in Mr F's shed

Crystal palace

Natural things

Wood pebbles

Developing the brief

Outdoor theatre for *Hamlet* by Anna Beer. The designer mapped the narrative of the play on to the site to develop the brief.

Ergonomic study

Outdoor theatre for *King Lear* by Ralph Saull. This ergonomic study of comfort, park etiquette and seating layouts for an outdoor theatre considers the experience of the user.

The student experience

This section charts the progress of a group of architecture students as they begin a 12-week design studio project and learn how to design for clients and users and develop a brief.

The brief

In week one the students were given a brief to design an outdoor theatre and actor's residence for a local theatre company in a public park. Each designer was to choose the identity of the actor and the inaugural Shakespeare play to be performed there. As with all architectural briefs, it was incomplete, allowing the designer to develop it and infuse it with their own interests and imagination.

Sketchbooks were used to record early observations, data and many different first ideas. Group tutorials were an important way for students to compare diverse and often conflicting observations, refine their own brief and make connections between different ideas, particularly between the brief and the play. Students were encouraged to question their assumptions and open up the possibilities of the project as widely as possible.

Students were encouraged to challenge the restrictions in the project brief, as shown below:

A space to sell tickets. A space for actors/musicians to change. A space to shelter the audience in wet weather performances. A space for the Actor in Residence to sleep, eat, wash, relax, change; also (optional) entertain guests and perform/rehearse.

The park itself should function as a free public open space and contain infrastructure/set design/landscaping to support performances. As the design develops, you need to make decisions on whether the facilities and infrastructure should be permanent, temporary or seasonal.

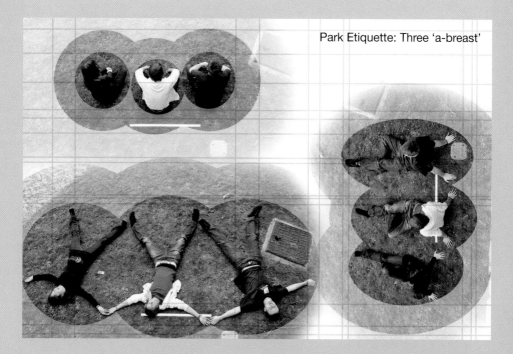

Park Etiquette: Three 'a-breast'

The client and users

The initial brief was provided by a local theatre company and the producer visited the design studio to discuss issues that were not covered or that were in conflict; to answer questions about how the company worked; to ask what the students' priorities were and what they hoped for at the end of the project. Site visits also improved understanding of what was possible and how the wider public would react.

Ralph Saull on making early design decisions:
The demand for distraction has prevailed this week. Procrastination at this stage is a sign that an idea is either fundamentally flawed, or still in such a stage of watery ambiguity that the task of putting pen to paper to solve it seems daunting. This game I play with the creative sphere of the brain ought to end in checkmate, the brain conceding that there is simply nothing else to do but work...

Rodolfo Acevedo Rodriguez on different uses of the site:
A solution to the spontaneous weather changes that can occur throughout the day: a jazz bar offers an outdoor stage for a local band and spectators; the cinematic space offers a similar indoor space transformed by means of mechanisms and technology.

William Fisher's ideas for designing the audience experience:
The idea for my theatre is to make the building camouflaged from view, so that the audience would have to rely on their other senses to find it, as if being blind [like King Lear]. This fitted in with my plan to bury the building, as the snow had buried the paths on site. The audience will have to rely on their hearing to find the theatre, as the music from the orchestra/buskers will spread throughout the park. Spent some time sketching down how the audience find their seat. Want to avoid the usual theatre experience where you see the rest of the audience and the set before the play starts.

Reality check exercise

For a studio-based architectural design project where there is no commission to design and build a building, and therefore no genuine accountability to a client, brief or site, the designer must use their understanding of these factors in a way that gives consistency to the project. If any of these factors are neglected or inconsistent with the others, flaws will emerge in the developing design.

Students were asked to carry out this exercise halfway through the project when they had the beginnings of a coherent proposal. It helps students learn how to develop a brief without compromising the creativity of their response to it. The exercise provides a check and balance mechanism to commit the designer to, and make them more aware of, the overall picture of the world that they have chosen to work within.

Construct a reality (however unreal) so that the total project is convincing within itself.

Many projects will have several competing and significant requirements. The architect must make critical judgements about their relative significance in order to deal with them creatively. Consider the needs and aspirations of the client, the public and the architect, in relation to the following issues:

cost	function	accessibility	quality
security	life cycle	users	usefulness
buildability	sustainability	maintenance	seasonality

1 Rank each of the issues in order of importance to the project.

2 Write a paragraph describing the consistent reality (however unreal) in which the project is set. Address each of the issues relative to their importance.

3 This written statement creates a more detailed and complex context for the project. Use it as a reference for future decision making as the project develops.

Clients, users and brief › Site, context and place

Typical activities at this stage

Site visits
Sketching
Surveying
Photography
Gathering information
Managing complexity
Collaboration
Site analysis
Mapping
Site strategy

Occasionally, through its location, resources or cultural significance, a site provokes a project to come into being. Most often, development is triggered simply by availability or the opportunity for re-use of a site. The demands of the site can transcend those of the client because every building, no matter how private, belongs to the public: its users include those who walk around it every day, whether they are invited to enter or not.

A single building is only a fragment of an urban, rural or suburban composition and will never be experienced in isolation. Therefore, it cannot be designed in isolation. The physical composition of a site contributes to making it a distinct place through the particular arrangement, type, scale and materiality of buildings or topography. Overlaid on its physical composition is a social, political, economic and cultural context, which influences the way that people use the site and which gives it its character. The character of a place is what distinguishes it from other places. This gives meaning to our experience of being there; it can inspire the users of the place and the architects asked to design there.

Our shared human reaction to a place is created by the dynamic of the physical site and its cultural context. This dynamic needs to be understood and interrogated by the architect preparing to design there. The information to be sought is tangible and intangible, objective and subjective. It ranges from the physical measurements and geology of a site to the atmosphere of that place at different times of the day or the emotional reaction of its inhabitants, perhaps to a significant event in the past.

The architect must visit, observe, participate in and record the site. Their perception must be heightened if they are to understand complex and subtle facts and reactions to the site that are not always expressed by the inhabitants. As with all complex architectural problems, the architect must use their critical judgement to discriminate and set priorities because an attempt to express all the characteristics of a place equally is likely to result in a shallow rendition or meaningless cacophony. The architect must pursue what seems most relevant and what they understand best. They must communicate in a way that leaves scope for interpretation and adjustment for change in the future.

CHORA

CHORA combines architectural practice and research into complex urban situations. These projects often involve large-scale projects on sites that face particular problems, such as very high-density living, climatic extremes or political sensitivity. CHORA's research laboratory was founded with the aim of understanding, modelling and transforming such places.

CHORA conducts research and develops methods of site analysis to produce urban studies into these places. They study both physical and non-physical qualities of each site, place the site within its larger context, and work with large and diverse client bodies to establish what defines it as a place now, and what should define it in the future, in order to bring about positive change.

In order to understand a site, its context and what defines it as a place, CHORA has developed an original methodology called 'Urban Curation'. This involves fieldwork to record urban conditions, the dynamic modelling of these conditions, the creation of potential scenarios for development, and the formation of proposals for policy-making and action planning. CHORA has also developed a planning tool called 'Urban Gallery'. This method and tool are currently being tested at London Metropolitan University and the Thames Gateway. Further applications are under preparation for the trans-oceanic corridor between Chile and Argentina, and the Taiwan Strait between Taiwan and mainland China.

A major outline of CHORA's methodology for urban planning in complex environments can be found in its book, *Urban Flotsam*. Raoul Bunschoten, the founding director of CHORA, teaches internationally and also runs student workshops that are associated with, and contribute to, live projects at CHORA.

Clients, users and brief › **Site, context and place** › Initial ideas

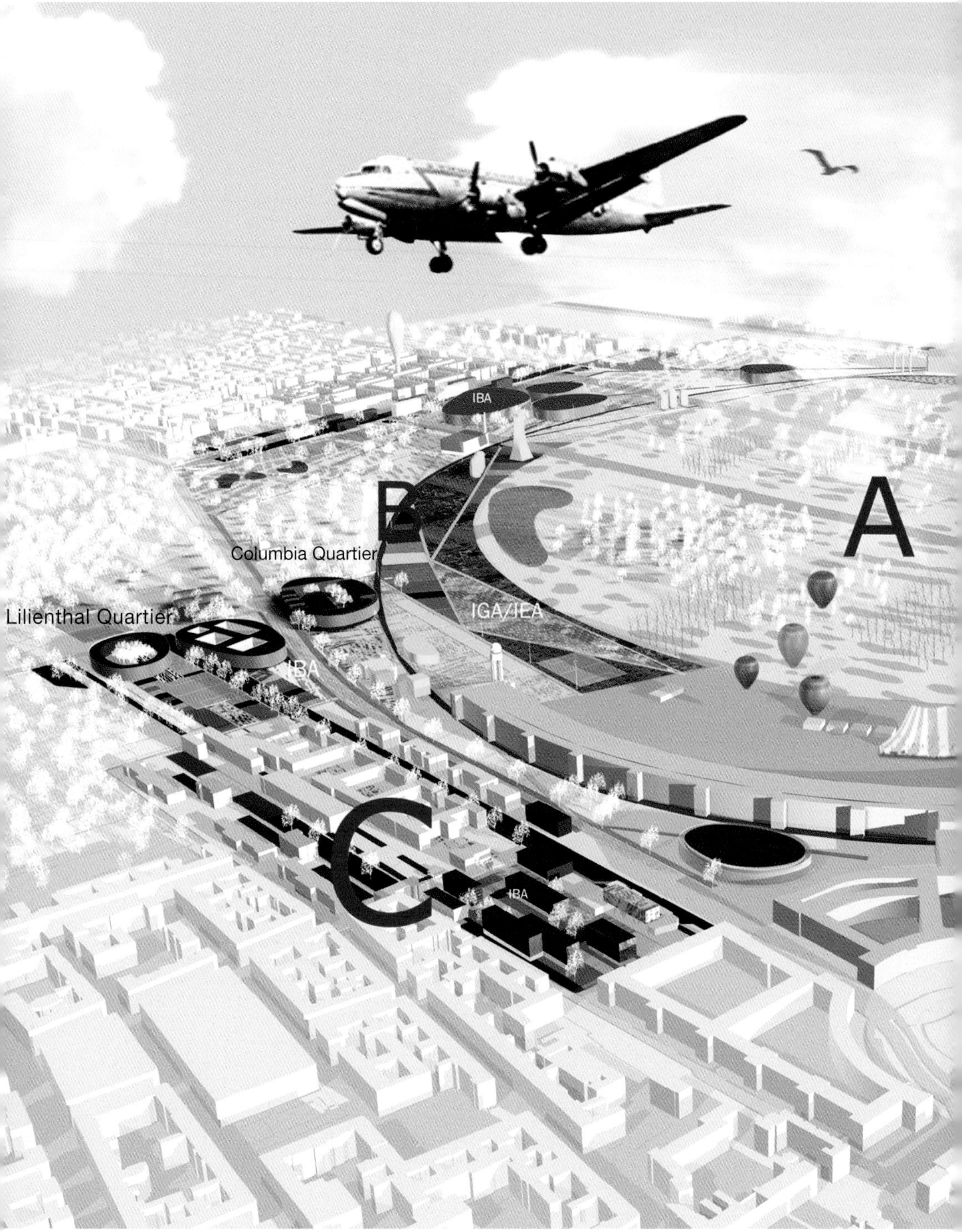

A

B

Columbia Quartier

Lilienthal Quartier

IBA

IGA/IEA

C

IBA

IBA

**Project: Tempelhof Energy
Incubator
Location: Berlin, Germany
Architect: CHORA
Date: 2009**

In partnership with Buro Happold,
Gross Max and Joost Grootens,
CHORA was one of the three
winners of the international urban
ideas competition for renewal of
the Columbia Quartier and the
former Tempelhof airfield in Berlin.
The economically viable and
sustainable proposals for the
50-hectare site will form the basis
of the master plan that will be created
by the new development agency
of Tempelhof. This competition entry
drawing shows the proposal in its
urban context.

Clients, users and brief › **Site, context and place** › Initial ideas

Project: Tempelhof Energy Incubator
Location: Berlin, Germany
Architect: CHORA
Date: 2009

This competition entry drawing must communicate to the judges the architects' understanding of the way that the site will be altered and used once the design has been implemented.

Interview with Raoul Bunschoten of CHORA

When you first visit a site, are there particular tools or methods that you favour to record your observations in the field?

There's no fixed way of experiencing a site. I think experiences can come to you in any way. It's always important to write and sketch. It's always good to put your own subjective observations through some kind of process, whether it's with pencil or whether it's through a few words or a mark on a map. Then it becomes available to analysis; it can be turned into knowledge. To communicate you have to use a language that other people use as well. Ultimately, if you want to sell your project you will have to explain why it's a good thing.

Site analysis is often presented as a study of static objects, such as the buildings around the site, but you are more concerned with the identification of mobile and dynamic phenomena. What can this tell us about a place?

We live in a world that is natural. You could talk about sea, earth, ground, the climate and all that's in motion: some of it moves very slowly, some of it moves fast. We live on the skin of the earth. It's dynamic and it's complex. Sometimes it moves very fast: like climate change. The second part of that concept is the way we live on this earth and I call that second skin of the earth. Humanity has created a total second skin of the earth, which consists of houses, cars, cities, information, infrastructures, oil, gas pipelines. Our second skin and first skin are both dynamic and they interact with each other and I think on any site that you go to, you always have to understand the relationships between these two skins. You always have to see the big picture, even if it is the long-term effect of climate change on a particular site or, vice versa, the conditions of the site. For example, take one small house on the site. The way that the house is designed, especially the way that the people manage their energy within that house, has an effect on the environment; the interplay between those two dynamic skins. Everything else that looks fixed – a house, a garden – is only temporarily fixed. That's where design has to happen. Design is about orchestrating the dynamics of the first skin and the second skin.

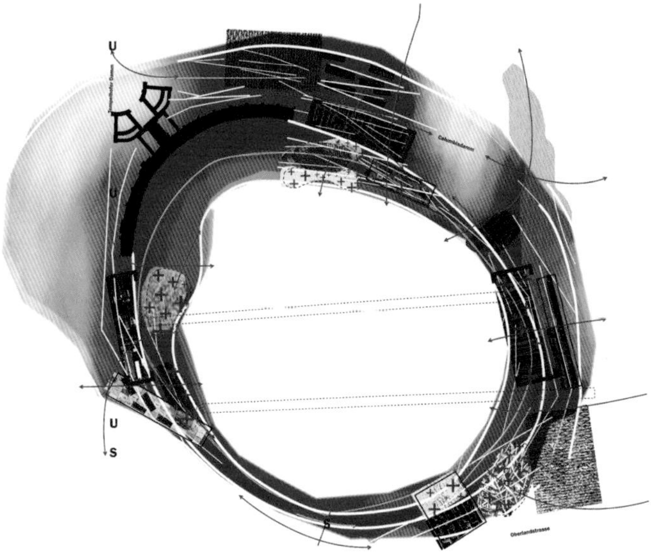

[53]

**Project: Tempelhof Energy
Incubator
Location: Berlin, Germany
Architect: CHORA
and Joost Grootens
Date: 2009**

above:
The Urban Gallery for Tempelhof
proposes changing the site in three
phases: initial landscaping and
opening up of the area to the
surrounding population; connecting
national projects like the International
Building Exhibition (IBA) and the
International Garden Exhibition (IGA)
to build and create experimental
housing; and the use of the site for
renewable energy regeneration and
linking up through intelligent systems.

right:
Plan of third development phase.
This site plan shows a proposal for
large-scale energy generation on
a currently redundant airfield site.

The design project

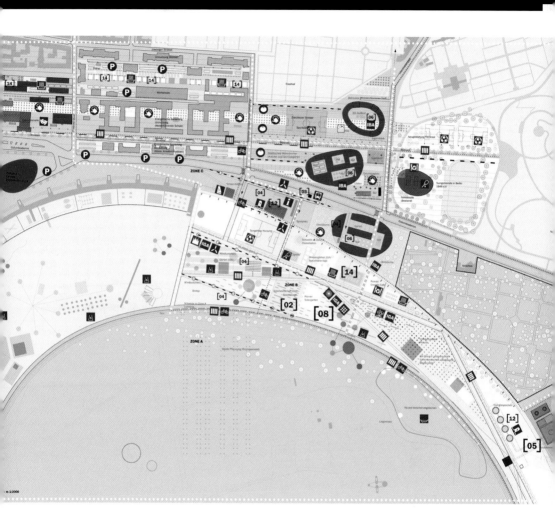

Project: Taichung
Location: Taiwan Strait
Architect: CHORA
Date: 2008

Mini-scenarios. CHORA asks participants to go out into the field to make observations and identify examples of four processes happening on site: Erasure, Origination, Transformation and Migration. These processes form a narrative called a 'mini-scenario'. These scenarios can be generated and used to describe the dynamic quality of any site.

Are architects well placed to be the people thinking about this?

Sometimes we think that we're not, sometimes we feel powerless. We think we cannot influence the large decisions; we're powerless against the decisions of a city planner, the politicians. But I believe we are not because architects are dreamers and at the same time we bring together utilitarian components and make them work. Look at [Andrea] Palladio: he looked at musical systems that created harmony in the universe and he tried to apply that harmony to the proportions of his buildings.

Would it be correct to say that when you visit a site you record close-up, on-the-ground findings, but when you're away from the site you are more focused on large-scale data, maps and statistical information?

On the site sometimes you pick a very detailed thing that you couldn't even imagine if you were away from the site. Over the years we developed a method, which was actually the start of our overall methodological approach that we have now. We start with a small exercise, which consists of a set of four processes that we try to observe. The four processes are like a filter and they are set in such a sequence that once the observations are made they form small narratives. We call them 'mini-scenarios'. It is something we use to mediate the subjective approach to the site into a more structured formulation, so that the experiences can be compared with each other. That's why it gets really exciting: if you go with a group of 20 or 200 people to a territory and each of them uses this device several times over, you get an almost instant weaving of narratives related to this territory.

Could you explain the four processes?

They are Erasure, Origination, Transformation, Migration. I developed them while having a walk with Alain Chiaradia. He was teaching with me at the AA [Architectural Association]. It's based on a metaphor to do with planting seeds in a garden. First you have the empty ground and you plant the seed, then the plant grows and reaches maturity, then the seeds float away in the wind. That's the metaphor but at the same time the processes themselves are a basic taxonomy, set up in such a way you could describe any kind of existing dynamic environment through [them].

Mini-scenarios

Xiamen and Taiwan flights + submarine cables

Typhoons + earthquakes

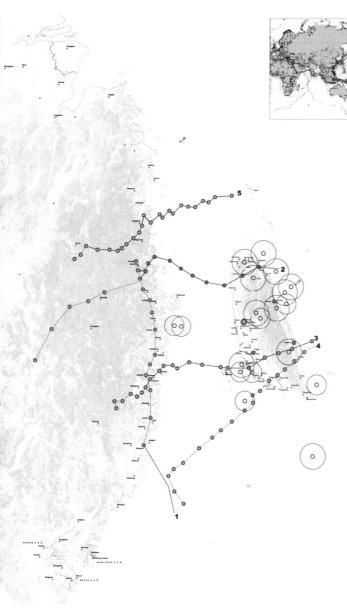

Project: Taiwan Strait Atlas
Location: Taiwan
Architect: Raoul Bunschoten,
Joost Grootens, Yuyang Liu,
Shuenn Ren Liou and Shao Sen
Wang with TungHai University
and Xiamen University
Date: Work in progress

Xiamen and Taiwan flights; typhoons and earthquakes. Mapping involves the use of graphical means to demonstrate connections between different types of data and phenomena. The Taiwan Strait project requires the analysis and understanding of complex issues such as political and climatic complexity, as well as high urban density design. CHORA's analysis put these issues together in context and proposed solutions to tackle the problems that they defined.

Clients, users and brief › **Site, context and place** › Initial ideas

Project: CopenhagenX
Location: Copenhagen, Denmark
Architect: CHORA
Date: 2002

Bean throwing on a map during
a project workshop. Despite the
random element that this introduces
to the process of site analysis, the
activity of the participants, who then
visit and observe the places identified
on the map, leads to a collective
knowledge about the site.

You also introduced a random element into your analysis of a site: throwing beans on a map.

The most difficult thing is to see things that you don't know are there and to get past the point where you see things that you expect to be there. That's why we introduced random processes, so you get to a point where you didn't imagine to be. Sometimes it's something that simply passes through as you observe, like a bird or a car. You can use a car to talk about transport or vehicles. It doesn't have to be profound, it can be banal. If you use this process as a group of people, you get a kind of collective intelligence. On the one hand you need the subjective experience because every single person has something meaningful to say about the world out there, but also you begin to get a kind of collective knowledge. One observation from a person can be linked to another observation made by someone else. The collective intelligence quickly represents the complexity of the site, especially a larger site.

To help understand the complexity of site data, you tend to frame portions of the site and make dynamic models.

The frame is an observational tool but it's also a choreographic tool. It selects and isolates in such a way that you can then say, 'Let's observe the dynamics in this field'. A site is not delineated by a legal boundary but by the frame you set. You decide what's in and out or what comes through the boundary and then you can say, 'I would like to see what's inside as a dynamic whole and I'd like then, in a model, to create a dynamic condition of what's inside.'

Are your scenarios an alternative to the approach of the conventional master plan?

Scenarios are whittled-down narratives, they are 'what if' situations. Scenarios are not about absolute outcomes, they are about pathways towards outcomes and possible connections. They are also ways of playing with reality. Scenarios don't offer solutions but ways of playing with the observations, the issues, the people involved. I would prefer master planning to be more like the work of a choreographer: a choreography of events and decisions over time and in space. There is a freedom about questioning reality and trying out different ways.

Architects are particularly familiar with the possibilities inherent in the existence of multiple solutions and the absence of one right answer.

A lot of people have to play with reality to test out different possibilities, to keep options open and even to learn about the flexibilities that we inevitably have to build in our environment. Society is changing very fast, so we have to learn that whatever we design has to be adaptive, has to be able to change. We should not be afraid of designing on a big scale. We should talk about it like an art form. That's why I talk about it as curatorial work. We can learn a lot from art disciplines. You can talk about beauty on a large scale.

Clients, users and brief › **Site, context and place** › Initial ideas

2010 PHASE I 2011 2012 2013 2014 **2015** PHASE II 2016 2017 2018 2019 2020

ACTIONPLAN

Das Diagram zeigt mögliche Programme und Projekte. Es zeigt auch die Wachstumsdynamik, welche sich aus dem Zusammenspiel der anderen 3 Ebenen ergeben kann.

SCENARIO

Das Diagram zeigt eine Übersicht der beispielhaften Szenarien welche in der jeweiligen Phase beschrieben sind.

2.Verknüpfung von Bildung, Forschung und Einwohnern

6. Nutzungsmischung und Baugruppen

5.Resilite Nutzungskonzepte

3.Kommunale Netzwerke

4.Verschärfte Gesetzeslage Innohalb des Inkubators

1.Beispiel eines Beteiligungsprozesses

Evolution der UGT

PROTOTYPE

Das Diagram zeigt eine mögliche Bandbreite von Pilotprojekten sowie Technologien, welche zu bestimmter Zeit eingesetzt werden können.

Stadt und Energie Inkubator [SEI.]

DATABASE

Das Diagram zeigt beispielhaft Informationen welche die Database bilden werden.

01 02 03

COP15 COPENHAGEN

04 05 06

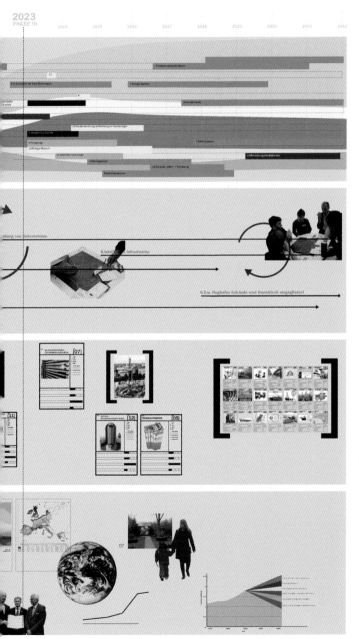

Project: Tempelhof Energy Incubator
Location: Berlin, Germany
Architect: CHORA
Date: 2009

The Urban Gallery was generated from an analysis of the site. It brings together site analysis data (bottom row); mini-scenarios observed on site (second from bottom row); and proposed potential scenarios (top two rows) to demonstrate a way to implement possible proposals for change.

Clients, users and brief › **Site, context and place** › Initial ideas

Can you give me an example of the scenarios that you created for the disused Tempelhof airfield site in Berlin?

There are two main scenarios for Tempelhof. One is the closure of an old airport that became famous because it was the first metropolitan airport in the world and because it was the site of the airlift that effectively saved the Berlin population from starvation after the blockade by the Soviet Union. So the first scenario is how to give it a new life as an infrastructure. The main aim is the mutation of the infrastructure into some other kind of infrastructure. We are interested in linking energy to city development. The second scenario relates to: 'Is a city a consumer of energy or can it become a producer of energy through our lifestyle?' This piece of city development could begin to perform like an alternative power plant. There are three phases. It starts in a very soft phase, which is mostly about landscaping and opening up the territory to the surrounding population. Secondly it's including large-scale national projects, like the International Building Exhibition and the International Garden Exhibition, which comes with funding to build and create experimental housing. The third one is to push for full-force renewable energy regeneration and linking up through intelligent systems. So those are the two scenarios combined. One is highly symbolic and historical and the other is highly utilitarian.

Project: Beckton Loop Energy
Incubator
Location: London
Architect: CHORA, Design for
London and Adams & Sutherland
Date: 2009

Scenario game. Game-like rules are introduced in order to structure the input of participants from different interest groups involved in the project workshop.

Interview summary

CHORA has developed a very particular methodology to analyse a wide range of sites, places and contexts. This method also feeds directly into strategies to make proposals appropriate to each place ('scenarios'). This means that site analysis becomes more than simply an exercise to help the architect to understand the place. The site analysis is designed to help the architect find a way to propose appropriate change in a place. It is particularly useful in complex, large-scale situations where there are many interested parties, several possible outcomes and no clear solution for the fundamental problems and conflicts at hand.

It is vital that any site is considered within its context and CHORA gives a satisfying weight to the invisible processes and phenomena on a site, which shape its context. These processes and phenomena may be invisible either because they are too large to see and understand in their entirety on site (such as a network of canals) or because they are intangible (such as the effect of an international economic subsidy on the choice of crop grown in a farmer's field). This willingness to embrace a global scale enables the architect to tackle significant issues and set ambitious goals for projects of any scale.

This does not mean that the small scale and the local are neglected. Local, first-hand observations are a fundamental part of CHORA's method. The multiplication of these observations through the collaboration of many individuals gives them a validity and depth that they could not otherwise have. The game-like structure set up for these observations lends an element of play and randomness to counteract the methodical nature of the site analysis; it allows participants to make both objective and subjective observations. The resulting scenarios build on the architect's creativity and ability to speculate on what might happen in the future.

Site plan

Outdoor theatre for *Macbeth* by Farah Yusof. This site plan was made by montaging a photograph of a physical site model, a map and a scaled site plan of the building proposal. This process has added several layers of information about the site to the final drawing.

Site sketch

Outdoor theatre for *The Tempest* by Jonathan Motzafi-Haller. This initial sketch of a sound wall was drawn in pen and overlaid on the existing photograph. This is an effective way to show an early idea in context.

The student experience

This section charts the progress of a group of architecture students as they begin a 12-week design studio project and learn how to analyse a site, identify the characteristics of a place and design a proposal for an outdoor theatre that considers the local and global context in which it is set.

The site

The site was located close to the design studio so that students could spend time there and make frequent visits to experience seasonal and temporal change. At the beginning, students had not yet developed the brief or made any design proposals so their efforts on site were focused on data gathering and absorbing the atmosphere. Students were asked to use objective methods, such as measurement in order to grasp the scale of the site, as well as subjective methods, such as drawing the atmosphere at a certain time of day. This improved their understanding of the physical facts about the site and the metaphysical qualities that distinguish it as a place.

Context

Students were encouraged to share information and compare interpretations of the site. They worked in groups to gather site data, interpret it and communicate it graphically at a review. They surveyed the land, trees and surrounding buildings; used light and sound meters; mapped the type and frequency of activity in the park; and researched the local climate, ecology, geology, culture and history. They then correlated the information in order to understand it better and put it to use in their own project. For example, a student who wished to design within the trees may link their knowledge of tree species, seasonal change and light levels to consider how the tree canopy and light quality of their building will alter from summer to winter.

SITE PLAN

Place

Students began to make initial proposals for their projects at two different scales. By looking at a very specific and local level, a designer can find the perfect site to observe the sun setting. By looking at a very general and global level, a designer can consider the journey of the theatre-goer from their home. This ensures that the designer reaches an understanding of what makes that particular place special and also has ambition for a project by seeking the potential for change on a larger scale.

U Ieong To on making sketches to record activity on site:
Sketches of the site are always my appetisers. They are sometimes what I see on site, and sometimes they are representations of what I feel on site. The sketches are also clarifying my intention and what I am actually thinking – they are transforming my perception of the site (which I see as a subtle matter) into something solid on paper. The challenge of this project is to design a theatre responding to the play as well as the context of the site. You just have to be an observer who studies everything – from the path of the ants on earth, the relationship between the trees and the birds, the atmosphere of the site, the behaviour of the people on site, the distribution of the trees to a wider context such as the topography, the flow of the people, the geometry of the site.

Rodolfo Acevedo Rodriguez on the potential of the site to provide the basis of an architectural concept:
There is a scene taking place where stages, characters and everyday objects can take part in a particular event that has the potential to be related to another. With connections we build narrative, linking one element to another. A building has the possibility of 'marking' a place, just like the leaf that decays on the ground, being there in the present and changing over time. A drawing is slightly different, it is regarded as a representation of what could be there in the future, but it is also a stain on paper, an evidence of a physical reaction that has taken place before.

Mapping exercise

Architects' observations of a site need to be a more analytical and heightened version of the way that the inhabitants of the place naturally absorb its qualities every day. To get the most out of a site visit the architect must plan ahead: what type of information is needed, what questions need to be answered?

The graphical language and techniques of maps are of particular interest to architects wishing to understand and represent data gathered on site. Maps represent particular types of data such as spot heights, landmarks or road types in relationship to each other at the same scale, normally in plan view. To retain legibility, a map also excludes data considered to be irrelevant for its purpose. The architect must make similar decisions about which aspects of a complex reality are most relevant to the project. Mapping this information enables the architect to find connections between significant elements of the project and deepen their understanding of the place.

Visit the site. In the area around the project site, record the location and appearance of:
1 An event that happens once at random during the site visit.
2 Infrastructure or other evidence of a process relevant to the function of the project.
3 An element that occurs frequently in the area around the site.

Pin a site plan on the wall and plot all of the observations on to it using pins, string, thread, found objects and cut-out representations of the elements observed. Photograph this mapping of the existing situation. Spend five minutes considering the patterns of use and inter-relationships between the elements observed.

Make one change. For example:
1 What if the event happened every month?
2 What if the infrastructure was removed?
3 What if the location of the elements were altered?

Rearrange the mapping to represent the change that is proposed and the way that the other elements would respond to it.

Typical activities at this stage

Concept sketches and models
Initial drawings and models
Testing ideas
Research
Understanding scale
Brief development
Opening up possibilities
Inspiration
Concept development
Happy accidents
Feedback
Managing complexity
Setting priorities
Collaboration

In the initial ideas phase it is important to keep possibilities open to allow innovative ideas to develop. Favoured solutions are explored through early sketches and models. The idea in the architect's mind and the one expressed by the hand need to be closely linked. Early ideas may be general but they are never complete; sketches and models are normally small in scale and have a certain looseness or vagueness. There are details to be resolved and connections to be made between unconnected or even contradictory ideas.

Some ideas will not be needed; others will evolve to serve more significant ones. This is necessary in order to manage the overwhelming complexity of the task. A little ambiguity of expression allows the gap between the mind and the hand to be acknowledged. The architect thinks, expresses the idea within the limitations of the media and reflects on the result before making a decision. Occasionally this looseness enables an idea to emerge like a happy accident: a small organisational diagram might have a textural quality that inspires an idea for the materiality of the building. The sketch itself triggers a solution that was not anticipated before it was drawn. Many projects make contradictory or incompatible demands that must be resolved through ingenuity or agreement of priorities. Initial ideas are experiments: they test the effects on the constituent parts of a design and the reactions of the client, architect and third parties.

Architects must gather project-specific knowledge on diverse subjects from the client's business practices to the water table on the site. There will be project reviews, meetings with the client, user consultations and negotiations with interest groups and government bodies, such as planners. The architect cannot rush to impose form on a project before reaching consensus on its meaning and purpose. This act of explaining the project to oneself, and to others, turns the idea of the project into a story. This narrative informs design decisions during the project's development and also gives meaning to the experience of those who will use the building.

Project: Hudson House
Location: Navan, Ireland
Architect: O'Donnell +Tuomey
Architects
Date: 1998

right:
Pencil sketch of elevation oblique
projection showing the volume of
the building.

far right:
Coloured pencil sketch of floor
materials.

O'Donnell + Tuomey Architects

O'Donnell +Tuomey Architects are based in Dublin, Ireland.
They have been involved with urban design, educational and
cultural buildings, houses and housing projects in Ireland, the
UK and the Netherlands. They have represented Ireland at
the Venice Biennale. Both Sheila O'Donnell and John Tuomey
teach at University College Dublin and lecture internationally.
Their work is characterised by the responsiveness of its form
to the site, its expression of a sense of that place, and a
materiality that emphasises the shell of the building. The
ambiguity of a shell – it could be either an unfinished or a
ruined building – communicates what the building is now and
also suggests what it could be in the future. This expresses
the process of architectural design itself, where an idea is
always restless and will continue to evolve until the architect
must fix it into form.

Project: Killiney House,
'The Sleeping Giant'
Location: Killiney, County
Dublin, Ireland
Architect: O'Donnell + Tuomey
Architects
Date: 2007

Watercolour sketches of site by
Sheila O'Donnell.

Interview with John Tuomey of O'Donnell + Tuomey Architects

What has changed after you have visited site for the first time?

When you come from site you have some kind of hunch formed in your head of the character of the project that you will propose. We would often be saying, 'This should be a garden or this should be an outpost or this should be a house dug into the site.' We would have some first thought independent of the technology or independent of the scale even. Actually, I don't think our first thought is material. I'd say that it is more to do with a kind of locational idea, like an anchoring idea that fixes the thought of the place.

So you give your projects names?

They are as useful to us as any diagram or any skeletal scheme or any type of conventional encapsulating motif that an architect will use. And we don't sit down and think, 'Now, what's the name of this one?', it's just that by the process of our conversation it emerges that something gets captured. I think Sheila and I are both interested in the idea that we'll discover something that we hadn't quite expected to discover.

We're actually both of us very analytical people but we're also using things like memory, analogy, intuition: thoughts that can't be legitimated objectively. There is some resonance that you wait for between the subjective interpretation and the actual conditions. To be satisfied you have to feel that not only do you feel it but it feeds back into itself and it becomes productive: 'If we are looking at it like this then that could lead us in this direction and that would be a useful way to go.'

How do you draw clients into this conversation?

I very often find that when we are coming to make a presentation of very early ideas, the work that is on the table is only the base layer to the understanding that is being communicated. You are trying to draw all of the participants into the possibility of what this project might be, which will speak back to their aspiration for it. So, if we suggest to the client that the project is a 'sleeping giant' and that doesn't resonate back, then it's not working.

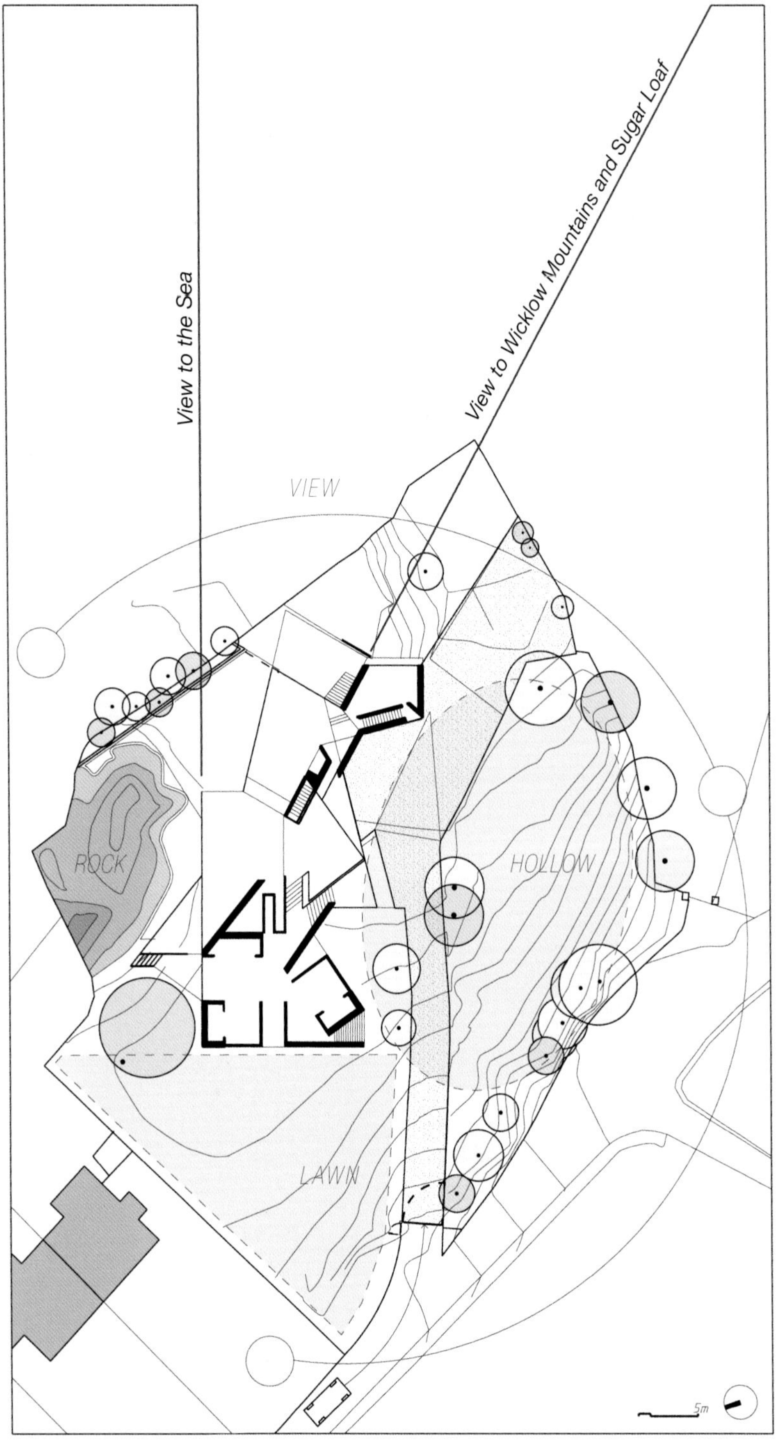

View to the Sea

View to Wicklow Mountains and Sugar Loaf

VIEW

ROCK

HOLLOW

LAWN

5m

The design project

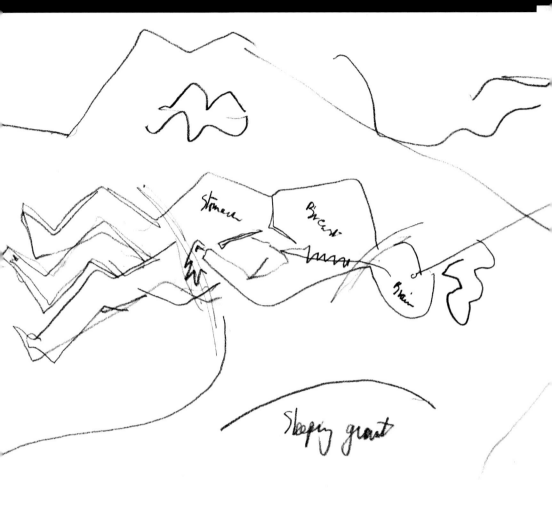

Stomach

Breast

Brain

Sleeping giant

**Project: Killiney House,
'The Sleeping Giant'
Location: Killiney, Ireland
Architect: O'Donnell + Tuomey
Architects
Date: 2007**

above:
Concept sketch showing the rocky
landscape as a reclining figure and
locating elements of the house
within it.

left:
Site plan showing the relationship
between the building and the
landscape.

How did it work with the Sean O'Casey Community Centre?

[There are] people who are very active in their own community – people who run the drama, sports and arts teaching and people who have a political sense of what a community centre should be. We have to meet them all and bring them into the idea of the project to help us to get the idea for the project. Somehow, the thought in the Sean O'Casey Community Centre was that the building would come down to the ground and be experienced by the pleasure and legibility of gardens. People could immediately begin to associate and identify with that. There are 1,800 houses in the East Wall, and they are all two-storey and they all have gardens. We were saying, 'Why wouldn't there be a garden in the house that belongs to everybody?'

We just came in with a white card model with four little volumes on it: a sports hall, a theatre, a plant room and an administration tower. They were four solids and then there were four voids, which we painted green; that is, four equivalent gardens. It is like we took these volumes out and the gardens got made. Now, it was a model about this size [palm-sized], you can put it in your hand. No evidence in it of anything to do with scale, windows, building, appearance.

It's a simple volume. We put that on the table, I promise you, everyone left that meeting knowing exactly what they thought they saw in that. Nobody asked 'What will it look like?'. Nobody asked any kind of end-result type questions. They all just wanted to know, 'Where does the idea come from and how will it feel?'

Project: Sean O'Casey Community Centre
Location: Dublin, Ireland
Architect: O'Donnell + Tuomey Architects
Date: 2008

top right:
Site sketch showing the massing of the surrounding buildings and the relationship between the two landmarks, the church and the community centre.

bottom right:
Diagram showing the relationship between different community functions (play/activity), building users (young/old) and the circulation routes between them (street/garden).

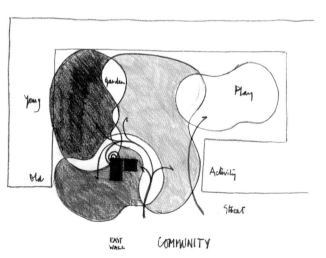

How did the idea for the tower emerge in that project?

Their brief to us was, 'We want a big building'. We kind of came around the back of them a few times and said, 'Well, pretty much everything that we understand about what you want this building to be belongs on the ground. If we were thinking about this from first principles it would be a single-storey building.' For us, the breakthrough came with this idea about voids: that we would make the gardens and replace the removed areas into volumes and that one of those volumes would be tall, like a little thumb sticking up. We would put their committee room, their powerhouse, at the top so that six storeys up they would have this view out and it would be as if they were in a very big building, but in fact the plot of that building is just the plot of a single house.

In your book, *Architecture, Craft and Culture*, you talk about architecture being a slow process.

We don't think slowly. We certainly don't act slowly. We make jumps but certainly sometimes you can be hanging around waiting for that click to happen. One moment of clarity is when you feel you've caught it: either named it or drawn it or diagrammed it or some way encircled it or captured it in your head. This is slightly precedent to having it solved but you know that you've got it. And then there's the satisfaction of going through a sketch design that begins to develop its own set of rules, where at a certain point you think, 'OK, it's not up to me to think this up any more. Now it's only up to me to follow the directions that are coming out of the thing itself.'

Project: Sean O'Casey Community Centre
Location: Dublin, Ireland
Architect: O'Donnell + Tuomey Architects
Date: 2008

right:
Tower and wall on St Mary's Road.

bottom right:
Palm-sized sketch model explaining the relationship of solid to void within the courtyard building.

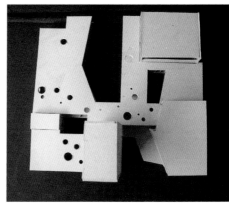

Project: Sean O'Casey Community Centre
Location: Dublin, Ireland
Architect: O'Donnell + Tuomey Architects
Date: 2008

View of entrance foyer and courtyard garden.

At the Glucksman Gallery in Cork you have said that you had to work very quickly and with only an outline brief.

They knew that they wanted an arts and culture building in that setting. They didn't actually know what the building properly contained. So we were participatory in the selection of the specific siting of the building. And in its programme and in its size. We moved so fast on it that actually it became very much led by its architectural idea. The invitation was: 'Build us a cultural building that will become a gateway between town and gown.'

I don't think that I'm being in any way disingenuous when I say that I think that it's only a re-reading of the site. I think that the take that we made on it is that this is a jump and this is interesting. So we said, 'We have to build it here because this is tarmac and everything else is grass. We won't disturb any living creatures. Then we will lift up into the trees.' And then we thought, 'How will we measure the space between the trees? Well, maybe then the building should be free within those trees, as if it is turning or something.' And that's where this idea came from about upriver and downriver and back to the college. It's like the building turns to see the city and then it turns again, and then it turns again.

Is there a connection between the free thought of the daydream or creative reverie and the architect's need to also make rapid decisions?

Deadlines! You wait until the last possible moment because you are afraid: 'If I do something today then I have taken away the possibility of starting it tomorrow.' As soon as you do something you've closed it down. Sometimes it's better to let it collect itself a little bit. But now I know it's very difficult to do that and it's impractical. Maybe through accumulated experience you have a feeling of knowing about something a little bit quicker. But I must say, I still enjoy the idea of having this thing in front of me that I'm only looking at sideways.

Project: Glucksman Gallery,
University College
Location: Cork, Ireland
Architect: O'Donnell + Tuomey
Architects
Date: 2004

View to river with gallery above. The gallery is placed high among the trees and appears to be tethered to the walkway below. This was inspired by an image from a Seamus Heaney poem about a celestial ship snagged on an alter rail.

The design project

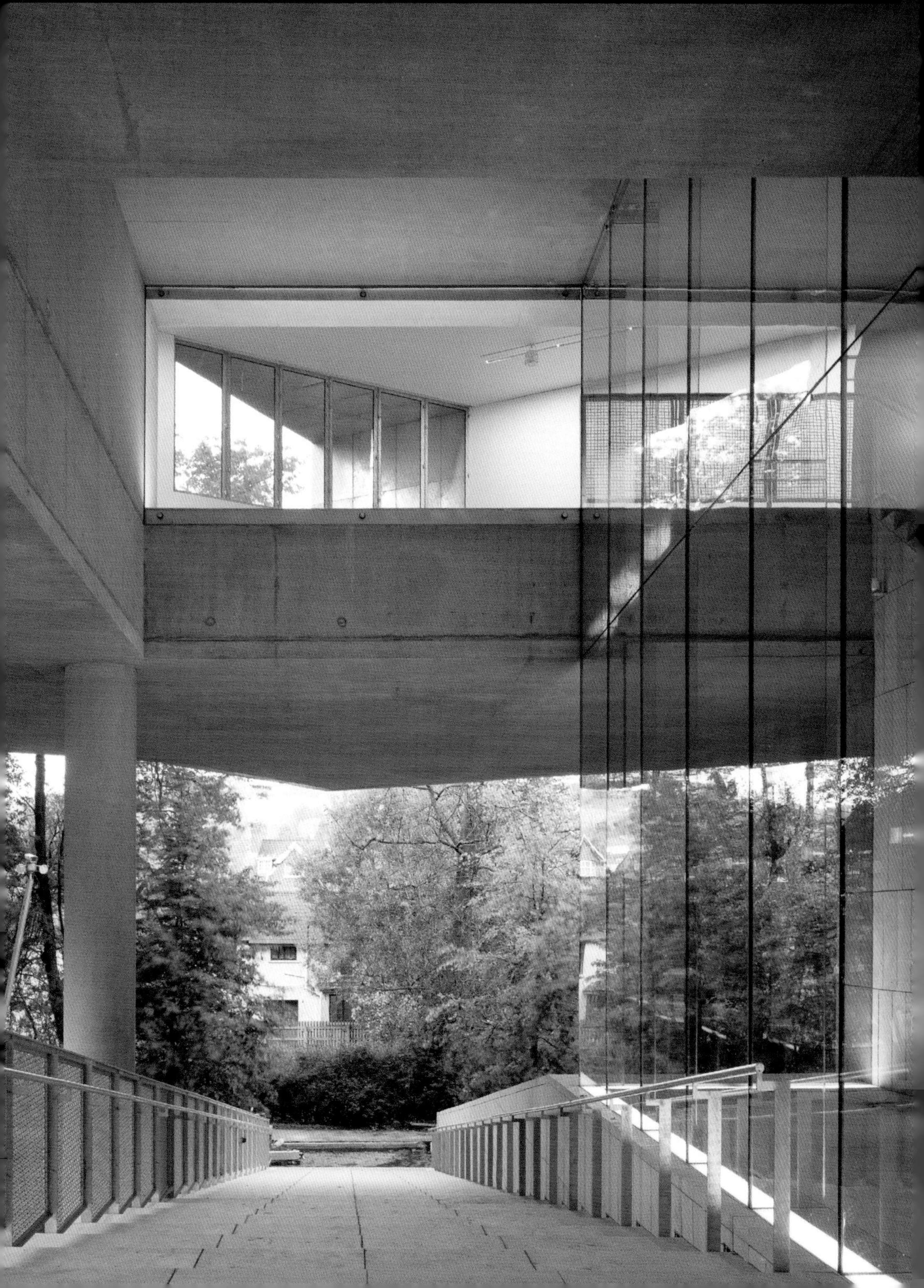

**Project: Glucksman Gallery,
University College
Location: Cork, Ireland
Architect: O'Donnell + Tuomey
Architects
Date: 2004**

above right:
Concept sketch showing the
connection between the ridge,
the gallery and the river.

far right:
View from the river.

The design project

How and when do you record ideas?

By drawing with pencil on paper continuously. Even to the
point that drawing can be removed from the paper, in the
sense that you draw it in your head or you draw with your
hands. But whatever you are doing in your head or with your
hands, it is drawing. Even making models is just drawing.
You're not drawing something that you've thought of already,
you're interested in seeing what comes out of the drawing.
In the process of that exploration the form emerges. There's
an exchange process, which is fascinating because the
drawing speaks back to you. That's the craft. It takes a long
time to learn that.

At a certain point you have to pull your head out of the
conflicting or insistent demands. Ask yourself what it's going
to be and what you're going to make of it. And actually, sort
of forget the problem. Fluency, as it is in language, is almost
below the level of consciousness. It's instilled in you and it
flows out of you because you have mastered it.

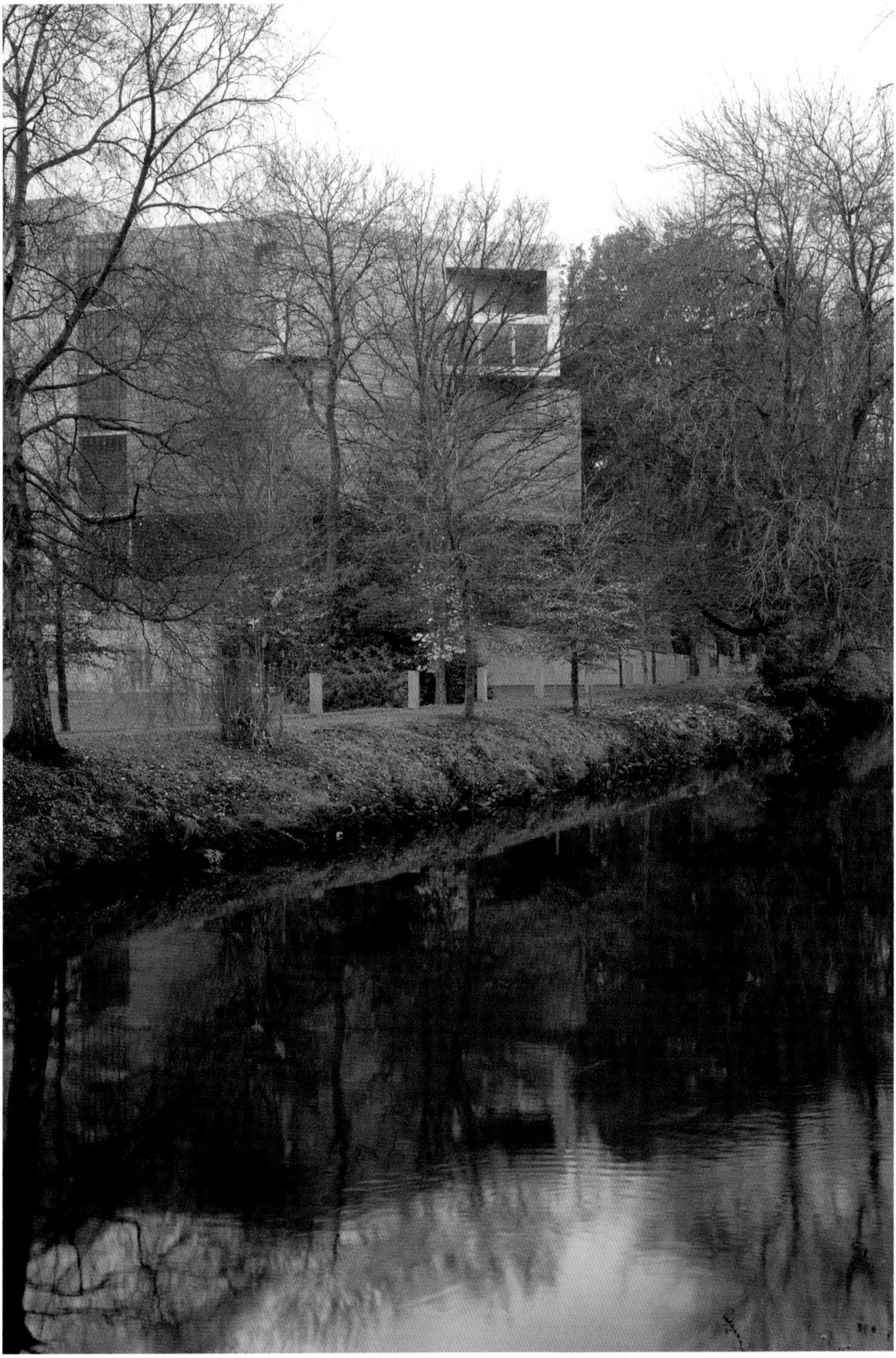

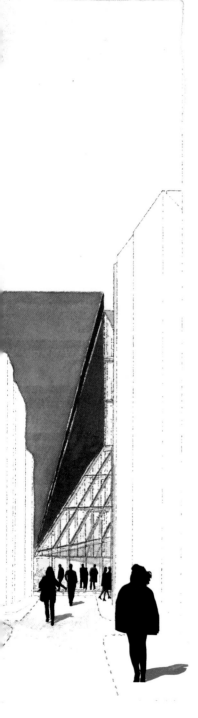

Interview summary

O'Donnell + Tuomey's considered architectural response to place is not dependent on the inspirational quality of every site that they work with; it is a consequence of their ability to see poetry around them.

Language and literature are not just sources of inspiration, they are also practical design tools. Before the direction of an architectural idea has been established or architectural form generated, words are used to collaborate within the office and with clients. Sketching, modelling and even physical gesture are treated in the speculative and flexible manner of a conversation: quick, explorative watercolour paintings; palm-sized, tiny sketch models; sketches on overlay paper passed between and drawn by many hands. Drawing is an act of design and exploration rather than a means of recording decisions made.

This openness to ideas, and testing them for their effectiveness, encourages creative reverie and inspiration. At certain points it provides an escape from the complexities and practicalities of the design problem at hand. The movement between reflection and action is particularly fluid during the initial ideas stage of a project. As John Tuomey says, 'I came across this term that Hans Arp, the Bauhaus artist used about his work: he called it his 'concretions', which I found a very satisfying terminology for a concept. A concretion: the making evident, the making substantial of something in form. Just as concrete cures and settles, it becomes hardened. I think concepts also pass through that same stage before they are made concrete.'

If an architect's mind is sufficiently nourished, by literature for example, their work will thrive and the richness of their ideas will be communicated to those who inhabit their buildings.

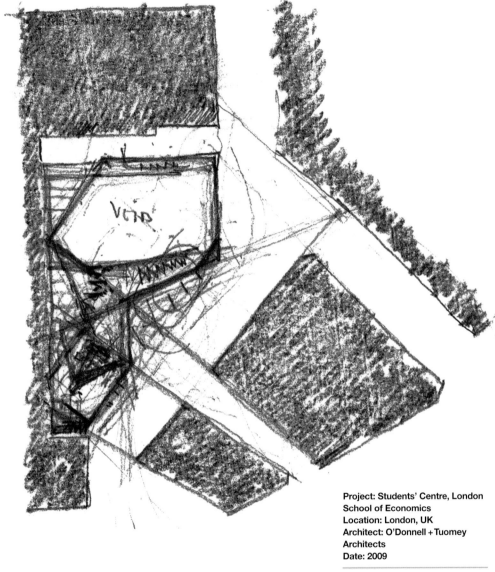

VOID

Project: Students' Centre, London
School of Economics
Location: London, UK
Architect: O'Donnell + Tuomey
Architects
Date: 2009

above:
Sketch showing routes and views to
and within the building; and the solid
and void both of the building and its
tight urban context.

left:
Watercolour sketch of the building
framed by tight streetscape.

Site, context and place › **Initial ideas** › Development and detail

The student experience

During the first six weeks of the 12-week design studio project, the students were asked to develop the client brief for an outdoor theatre and to analyse the site. Their response to this generated initial ideas that were developed into sketch design proposals.

Initial ideas

At the beginning of a project it is necessary to develop the brief and understand the site while also searching for ideas that will provide the basis for an architectural concept. The students were asked to make a small stage-set model of the site and place their chosen Shakespeare play in that location. By choosing a play the students were able to introduce an element of their own interests as designers. This task linked the available factors that could form the basis of an emerging architectural concept: the brief, the site and the designer's own sensibility. By finding a concept that is relevant to the constraints and possibilities of the project, the designer is able to turn these factors into something positive that will also help them to choose from the multiplicity of possible directions at the initial ideas stage.

Without a willingness to think the unexpected it is very difficult for a designer to generate creative ideas and test the potential and ambition of the project. Some students enjoy the multiplicity of possible design directions and generate many creative proposals (but can find it difficult to commit to an idea when deadlines loom). Other students find this stage uncomfortable and this spurs them on in the search for a brilliant solution that they are satisfied with (but may need to reject later on in favour of a better one, having worked hard on the original solution).

Students were encouraged to record and reflect on their design decisions; each designer began to experiment with different design methods and tools such as diagrams, modelling and film making in order to develop their initial ideas into design proposals. At the interim review, students presented process work and showed the proposal to scale in context. This was an important opportunity for students to recognise the potential of their project to develop fully through further iteration.

right:
Journey model montage

Outdoor theatre for *A Midsummer Night's Dream*, by U Ieong To. This early sketch model, describing an idea for the journey through the building, has been montaged on to a conceptual drawing describing the sound and atmosphere of a performance on site.

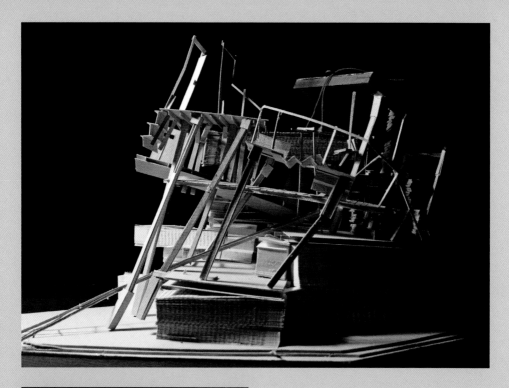

above:
Sketch model

House of Romeo by Rodolfo
Acevedo Rodriguez. This sketch
model, made using second-hand
books, records the intention to use
the play as a basis for the design
concept. The books also open
up ideas of texture, weight and
materiality; some intentional,
some discovered.

Site, context and place › **Initial ideas** › Development and detail

Holly Newnham on the concept behind her project:
I wish to explore the idea of control and manipulation that runs throughout the play. Characters are hidden, secrets and lies are revealed and things are seldom as they seem. My initial ideas explore the physical realities of these themes through a stage set that allows visible change through the duration of the show: a rotating stage where characters can be concealed, a timber structure with varying levels and openings. At the moment it is too static and I strive for a design that responds to its open air surroundings.

Ralph Saull on the use of diagrams to explain ideas:
Design by diagram: developing a diagram which summarises the design is necessary for sustaining direction, but is it inhibiting? Does it act as an intrinsic veto vote against original thoughts that at an earlier stage may have made the mind swim with possibilities? Perhaps this aide-memoire acts as blinkers to the creative mind. If you didn't wear them it is likely that you would end up with a mass of ideas, each only pursued as far as they held their novelty.

Anna Beer describes the use of a modelling method to analyse the site that inspired the form of the building proposal:
Exploring the possibilities of a loom, changing material, tension, boundary widths, and rhythm. Although the loom models were just for experimenting, I started applying certain characteristics of the site to them: Boundary A was a constant, fixed rhythm representing the fence on-site; B was a variable. I had in mind that in relation to the site, these random points might represent trees.

Journey model exercise

During the initial ideas phase, the site and brief provide a vast amount of information. The architect must spend time discovering which elements to prioritise and develop. One possible technique is the journey model, which prompts reflection on the nature of the journey to the site and encourages the qualities of this experience to be continued within the site and the building itself. This technique can be used to make legible first proposals for internal space without any need to design a fixed external form: no enclosure or shell is required to understand the sequence or nature of the spaces. You will need recycled scrap model-making materials and/or found materials brought from site.

1 **Remember** (5 minutes): From memory, recall the journey to the entrance of your site. Write down any significant features of the route, landmarks, topography, materials, events, sounds and so on.

2 **Make** (15 minutes): Starting from the point in your journey where you could first see your site, make a sketch model of the journey to the site. This model should link the significant features of the route (see 1) and represent your impression in abstract and not to scale.

3 **Record** (5 minutes): Photograph the model.

4 **Reflect** (5 minutes): Stand, lift up the model and look at it from every angle, thinking about what this series of spaces could be.

5 **Adapt** (15 minutes): The sketch model must now be adapted to represent the possible journey within your project proposal/building. First, decide at what point along the journey you should set the entrance threshold (is it immediate or is there a build-up to it?). Next, begin to bend, twist, break and separate the model to represent the different spaces within your proposal and their relationship to each other.

6 **Record** (5 minutes): Photograph the model and annotate with a description of the nature, function and sequence of spaces that you have created.

Typical activities at this stage

Scaled drawings and models
Design resolution
Detailed design
Materiality
Research
Decision making
Execution of concept
Samples and prototypes
Feedback
Control
Managing complexity
Collaboration

Once issues such as the scale, function, materiality and concept of the proposal have been resolved in outline, the architect will begin to make certain key decisions; these decisions influence others that are apparently less strategic. The complexity of any architectural project means that it is necessary to 'fix' some ideas in order to explore the consequences. It is important to remember that these choices are only paper decisions and can easily be reversed if necessary, often without destroying the integrity of the whole scheme. Revisiting and interrogating should reveal possibilities that can enhance the concept and even the detail. This process ensures that the design of form and space is tested. A form that is chosen at the beginning of a typical project and does not alter during the design development is unlikely to have been very closely questioned by its designer; it lowers the ambition for the project.

Drawings and models increase in scale and bring together many different elements of the design, ranging from the activities of the users to the structural strategy. Drawings relate different elements to one another and resolve any difficulty in bringing them together. Information from consultants and specialist sub-contractors (such as services engineers and pre-cast concrete manufacturers), appears within the architect's drawings. The architect must coordinate this advice and collaborate with consultants to make strategic design decisions that retain the clarity of the concept. The form designed by the architect creates an envelope and a series of spaces that must be designed in detail so they can be constructed. The way that materials and elements are joined together at this scale can be as poetic as the sequence of form and space, despite the pragmatic realities of the materials concerned. The concept can be expressed right down to the last bolt.

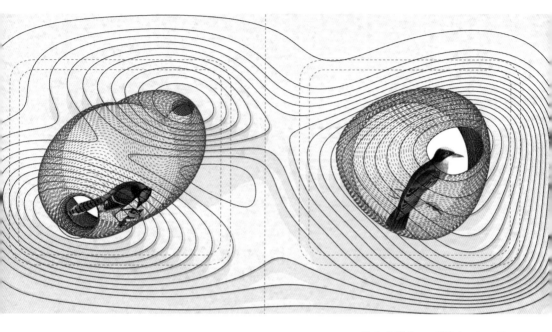

**Project: 'Urban-est' bird and small
animal habitat
Location: New York
Architect: Snøhetta
Date: 2009**

Detail of single module. This project
adapts a standard masonry unit to
provide a habitat and observation
place for birds and small animals. It
provides a sculpted, inhabited façade
within the city.

Initial ideas › **Development and detail** › Construction and occupation

The design project

Project: Tubaloon
Location: Kongsberg, Norway
Architects: Snøhetta
Date: 2005

An inflatable temporary bandstand
for an annual jazz festival.

Snøhetta

Snøhetta is an integrated landscape, interior and architecture practice based in Oslo, Norway, and New York, USA. The practice is known for its international cultural projects, many of them large in scale, complexity and cultural significance. All of its work, whether large or small scale, retains a strong link between landscape and architecture, and demonstrates the importance of architecture's social dimension. The site and context for every project are considered to be unique, which is a major inspiration for Snøhetta's design work. The directors, Craig Dykers and Kjetil Thorsen, teach in Oslo, New York and Innsbruck and they lecture internationally.

Many of Snøhetta's projects are culturally, technically, spatially and programmatically complex. They require the involvement of many different individuals and organisations, from politicians to pest control. The New Opera House, Oslo, completed in 2008, is part of an urban transformation of Oslo's waterfront. It is the workplace for approximately 600 employees from more than 50 professions. It took ten years to plan, fund and build the $750 million structure, which has a floor area of 38,500m^2 (415,000 square feet).

The Tubaloon is a sculptural band shelter for the Kongsberg Jazz Festival in Norway. The textile structure is a hybrid of lightweight steel tensile members and pneumatic beams, which can be easily stored and installed in a couple of days, ready for the annual festival.

The National September 11 Memorial Museum Pavilion will be a cultural institution on the site of the former World Trade Center in New York. The design and programme of the building have been subject to many revisions as political pressure and public sentiment adjust their intentions for the sensitive site. The current evolution of the design will function as an entrance connecting the Memorial at street level with the exhibition space below.

**Interview with Craig Dykers and Kjetil Thorsen
of Snøhetta**

**You have experience of working at many different scales
and have said that a family of five could be as complex
as a city. What are the advantages in your design process
of making such a conscious link between the scales?**

Kjetil Thorsen
You move towards organising elements in relationship to
each other, they start talking together.

Craig Dykers
It's very difficult to imagine things as they may appear in
reality, as they will be when they're completed; so going back
and forth between scales allows you to move more freely
between the built environment and the imagined one. So
in that sense I guess there's no such thing as a real scale.

Kjetil Thorsen
But scale is a difficult issue, because depending on the
distance to the object, obviously scale changes. It changes
in relationship to where you have your eye. If you look at
a city from the plane it might be a living room; so scale often
is portrayed at the level of content it has, relating to how
close you might be observing it. You could also say that
objects change scale in themselves depending on where
you are located.

**Comparing two projects: the Tubaloon and the Opera
House, which have similar purposes but are very different
in scale, would you say that one was more complex than
the other?**

Kjetil Thorsen
The difference of complexities is defined by the way one
simplifies a task. It is not the way you're looking for inherent
complexities but how you try to solve these complexities in
the simplest manner. In that sense, large-scale and small-
scale projects don't differ. Maybe large-scale projects allow
you to experiment more, simply because the economy
follows the size of the project. This experimentation demands
more design process control because it is more difficult to
maintain a thread throughout the process. The Tubaloon took
four months, so it doesn't allow you to change your mind
while you're doing it.

Initial ideas › Development and detail › Construction and occupation

**Project: Norwegian National
Opera and Ballet**
Location: Oslo, Norway
Architect: Snøhetta
Date: 2008

above:
Main theatre with the stage curtain
designed by artist Pae White to give
a three-dimensional appearance to
a flat woven textile.

right:
Plan and long section of the opera
theatre set in its immediate context.

What's the best way you've found to retain conceptual clarity in a project like the opera house?

Kjetil Thorsen

By a new word we have invented: simplexity. Maintaining
conceptual ideas is to put up a set of rules that everyone
follows up to a certain point. We had an intention in the
Opera never to have more than three materials meet in a
detail. If you use a material, use it to its largest extent but try
to reduce the use of any other materials. The form might be
complex, but the way you solve the form might be simpler.

Craig Dykers

Certain parts of the project may have to be diminished in
one way or another to allow other parts to grow, depending
on where you're putting your emphasis. If you don't think
through that idea wisely in the very early stages of the
project, the whole thing can fold because there's simply
not enough traction in all the different materials and choices
to allow the project to move forwards.

Kjetil Thorsen

Also not trying to put all your ideas into every project.
Limiting yourself to the development of long-term design
issues is more important and that gets easier as you mature.

The design project

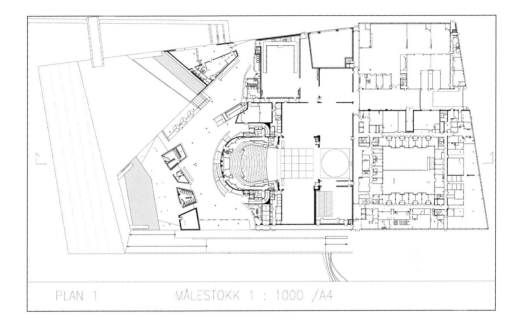

PLAN 1   MÅLESTOKK 1 : 1000 /A4

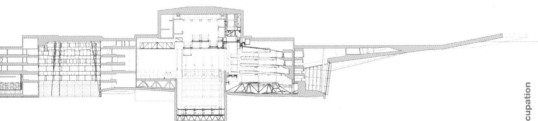

Does your trans-disciplinary approach help maintain the clarity of design development?

Craig Dykers

It's not about the fact that different disciplines are interacting, it's about not knowing which discipline belongs to which cultural or academic route.

Kjetil Thorsen

I think the design process starts very much before that. I think it starts by analysing the situation, site and environment. The next phase is usually a lot of talking and not drawing so much. If we draw, it's diagrams, trying to explain certain settings, which we find from a more subjective way of looking at the analysis. After a lot of talking you start sketching. That's why we sometimes don't say we design projects, you know; they sort of grow in a group, during meetings without agendas.

Craig Dykers

The creative process sometimes needs to allow for ad hoc or surprise directions to occur. Nothing should be considered particularly stupid. Everything should be considered important and you have to move through the ideas in order to determine if they're applicable or not.

Kjetil Thorsen

It's like a funnel. You start really quite wide; as you get towards organising the project you funnel it through this process and it gets tighter and tighter.

Craig Dykers

It's very easy to be reliant on your personal or cultural baggage, so to surround yourself with people of different backgrounds, academically or culturally, helps you to question your own directions.

Project: Norwegian National Opera and Ballet
Location: Oslo, Norway
Architects: Snøhetta
Date: 2008

above right:
Open day for the public during construction, showing the use of the roof of the building as a public promenade.

below right:
Conceptually the Opera House is divided into the back stage (the factory) and the public spaces (the carpet) by a timber screen (the wave wall) along the shore line.

The design project

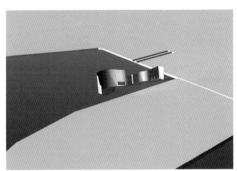

The wave wall

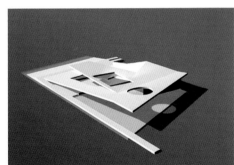

The carpet

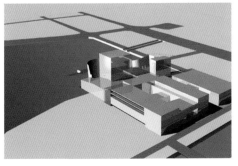

The factory

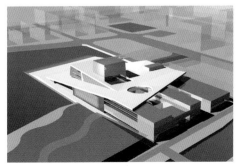

The three elements combined

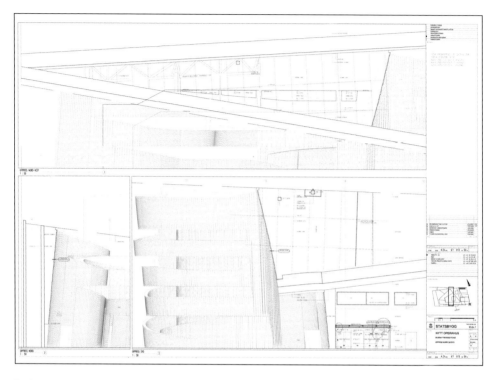

**Project: Norwegian National
Opera and Ballet
Location: Oslo, Norway
Architects: Snøhetta
Date: 2008**

above:
Detail drawing of the timber wave
wall between the public space and
the theatre spaces. This drawing
would be used to communicate
its general arrangement to
the contractor.

right:
The timber wave wall between the
public space and the theatre spaces.

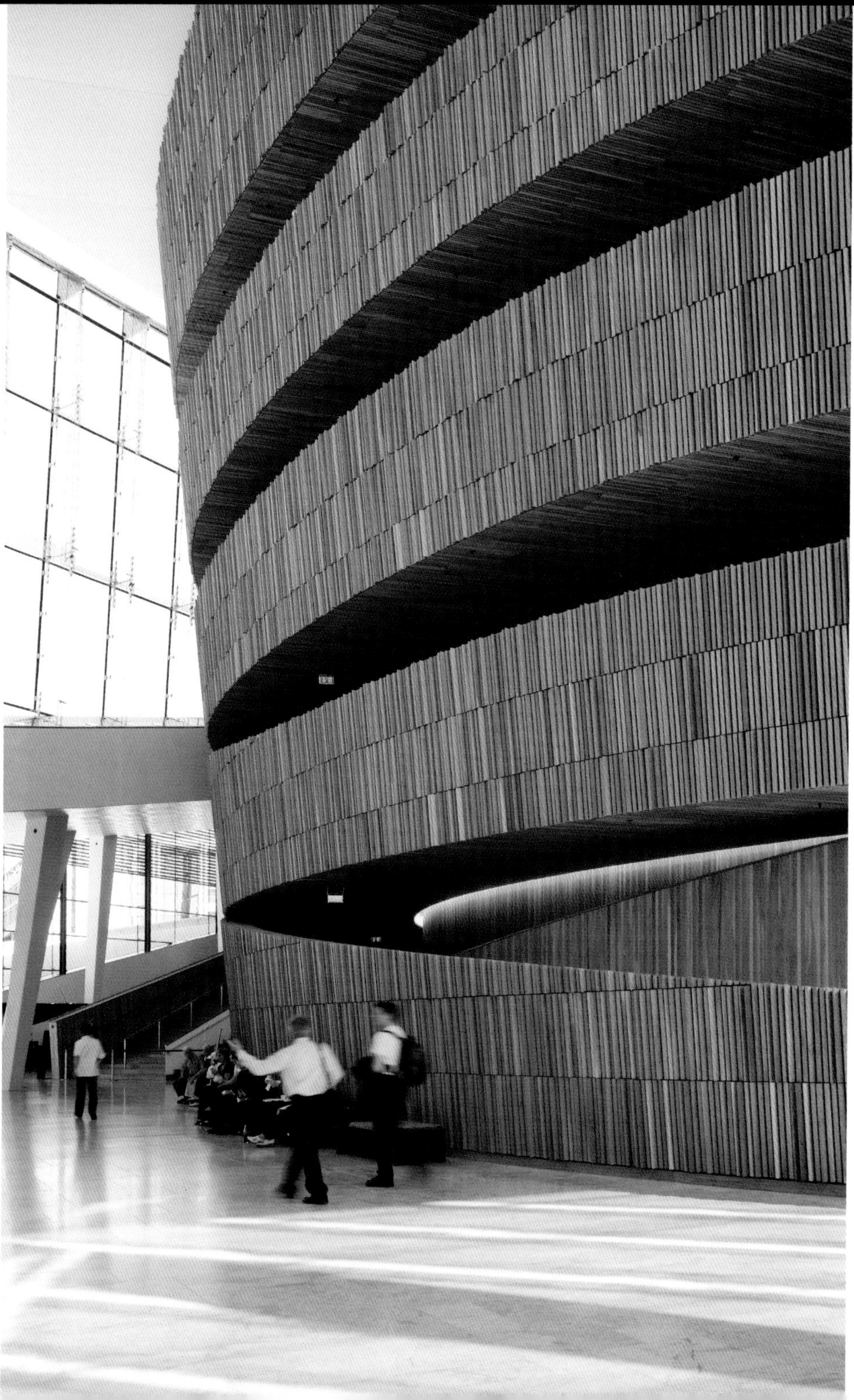

**Project: King Abdulaziz Centre
for Knowledge and Culture
Location: Dhahran, Saudi Arabia
Architects: Snøhetta
Date: Ongoing**

above:
Early conceptual model of tubular
steel shading wrapped around the
pebble form of the building.

right:
1:1 mock-up of part of the tubular
steel shading and glazing layers;
this is used to test the design,
manufacture and performance of an
important element of the building.

**You have said that the people who architects design for
are not abstractions.**

Craig Dykers
People are often pulled out of the picture; at least, people
as living creatures. They're normally codified into some
functional analysis.

**The point where a practising architect often loses that
thought is once they're detailing and they've got
something like a door schedule to do. How do you
protect against this problem?**

Kjetil Thorsen
Scale models and mock-ups: for instance, where you have
to walk through them or you have to touch them. So by
making things which move under your skin, really moving
you, you have to be concerned about the human condition.
If you consider only form then you would be very quickly lost.

Craig Dykers
Also, the notion of discussion doesn't die as the project
moves forward, so in terms of associative issues we're often
re-envisioning our understanding of an object. There are
discussions quite late into the process that say, 'Well, we
didn't realise it but this thing actually is doing something else
to the general population as opposed to what it started out
to do', and you make adjustments to your thinking.

Kjetil Thorsen
We talk about how you sit or how you lie, how the night
looks, how the day looks when you walk through.

What piece of work tends to prompt a re-think?

Kjetil Thorsen
Realising a mistake!

Craig Dykers
Anything to do with a vision of something in three dimensions. You rarely talk about buildings in the actual abstract, which is two dimensions or less. I suppose it's when you're seeing your building and walking through it and being able to understand what it's like to actually be in it.

Kjetil Thorsen
If you have only a concept, you tend to follow that through. If you have only the details and the material you tend to follow those through. Say you start at both ends at the same time and try to merge them in the middle somewhere, then you're more likely to have carried with you both of these elements, instead of starting at one end and believing it's a one-line sort of thing that is happening. The building needs to have a real performative aspect to it, which means, in our terminology, that it has to come back and claim something.

Craig Dykers
In general, architects and the architectural process could be opened up to other disciplines to allow for varying perspectives. We try to do it as much as we can: invite authors or screenwriters or artists, especially with public art and cultural projects. It allows for a change in perception.

Could I ask about the National September 11 Memorial Museum project? There must be so many different people, opinions and pressures to accommodate.

Craig Dykers
We started our practice after winning the Alexandria Library commission, which in many ways has a similar foundation. It was about loss, the loss of history and the loss of valuable cultural material. The Library was about an international institution that united people from around the world to work together and it was about transforming a society after some kind of tragic loss had occurred at a historically prominent location.

Kjetil Thorsen

For this project we were more specific at the beginning: developing it through negotiations and discussions with a lot of different people and that was a mindset.

Craig Dykers

I think the only way you can do that is to have a balanced capability of architectural skill and skills in human relations. They are able to talk to us. That doesn't mean we don't have strong opinions but at least we can find constructive ways to move forward.

Kjetil Thorsen

Where the cultural differences are big, we try to look for similarities rather than the differences; it makes it easier to move forward but it doesn't devalue the issues at hand.

Craig Dykers

We also function generally within the office in the same way. At a smaller scale in the design process we're already dealing with those same issues; so someone sitting across the table and someone sitting next to you are going to have occasionally conflicting ideas and we're trying to work that out.

What techniques do you use to cope with complexity while you're designing?

Kjetil Thorsen

Having a great idea, and being afraid of ruining it by creating it, is maybe the biggest and most difficult jump of all creative processes. Sort out the correct tools. Hand sketches, drawings, computers, models, digital model-making, hand model-making, music, reading, dance, performances; whatever you have. I think to get a grip on these things is to bridge between carrying, being pregnant with something and then actually giving birth.

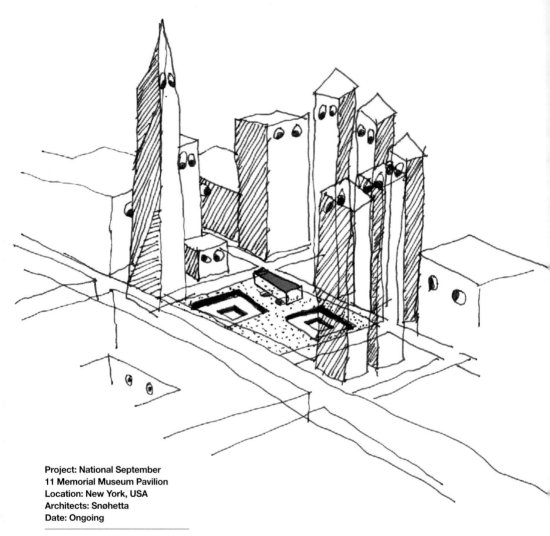

**Project: National September
11 Memorial Museum Pavilion
Location: New York, USA
Architects: Snøhetta
Date: Ongoing**

above:
The museum is the only building on
the Ground Zero site and will be
surrounded by large-scale buildings.
This sketch conveys the awareness
of the architect that they are being
watched; not only by the public and
the government but also by the
architects designing the neighbouring
buildings and their clients.

right:
Digital representation of current
proposal.

The design project

Interview summary

The willingness of Snøhetta to embrace duality and see a situation from an opposite perspective is a driver for, and result of, their collaborative, discursive approach to architectural design. Both within and outside the office, debate is a creative act. The public and sensitive nature of several of their buildings demands this. One suspects that they refuse to be precious about ideas. The range of their development work shows that they explore ideas in many different media and use new technology to test their work.

Architects can fall into the habit of seeing design as a broadly linear journey, with decisions being made from an initially large scale until they reach the precision of detail design. By maintaining an awareness of the tactile and the human scale throughout, and simultaneously considering the social and the global scale, Snøhetta, with their 'trans-disciplinary' approach, retain a clarity of concept that is communicated in the finished building. Complexity is kept in check where appropriate: detailing in the Opera House dictates that no more than three materials meet. Their conception of scale as a relative experience rather than a hierarchical order means that ideas can be communicated on many levels.

They describe the importance of the 'performative' quality of their buildings and open them up to be tested and experienced as widely as possible. The roof of the Opera House is designed as a public space that links the city back to the fjord and the hills. This requires the architect to resolve technical issues, such as designing a surface that is safe to walk on while also enabling the walker to experience the poetic qualities of the journey from water to sky mapped out by the roof. The interrogative development of the design and the tactility of building details are symptomatic of their interest in the human condition.

Project: National
September 11 Memorial
Museum Pavilion
Location: New York, USA
Architects: Snøhetta
Date: Ongoing

Initial study model for the façade. Natural light was used to create constantly changing prismatic patterns.

Initial ideas › **Development and detail** › Construction and occupation

Materials study

A Midsummer Night's Dream, by U leong To. The materials, their quality, source and application have been represented in this study.

Model montage of tea house

Outdoor theatre for *Romeo and Juliet* by Rodolfo Acevedo Rodriguez. In order to best represent the reality of the project on site before it has been built, the designer montaged a model on to site photographs.

The student experience

This section describes the activities of a group of architecture students during the last six weeks of a 12-week design studio project. At this stage they were expected to develop their design for an outdoor theatre in detail.

Development

At the interim review each student presented their process work (early sketch ideas and analysis) and orthographic drawings of their proposal to scale and in context. This allowed the visiting critics and fellow students to understand the proposal, as well as the reasoning behind it, and to give feedback. The discussion focused on ways to develop successful ideas further; strategies to edit projects where too many ideas were making them confusing; issues to consider that had been neglected; and advice on whether to reject or rethink ideas that were flawed.

Students were encouraged to increase the complexity of their initial proposal. They tried different design tools and used overlay paper to work on their existing drawings. Design was interrogated at small scale ('where should the entrance to the building be located?') and large scale ('what route will the audience take to arrive at the theatre?'). Students were asked to develop and use their concept to bring hitherto unconnected elements together.

Detail

Students' ideas about materials had begun to form early on through model making, drawing and from looking at built precedents. They were also able to use their knowledge of structures, environmental science and construction to help to answer questions raised by their project (such as, 'how will it stand up?'). Each designer was encouraged to develop certain areas in more detail, focusing on those that were best understood and most closely related to the concept (for example, 'in a project about light, how should the windows be designed?'). The resulting design detail informed further design work on the rest of the building, which in turn informed further decisions. It was also important to learn that technology, which can be viewed as a constraint, also has the potential to generate architectural concepts.

ACT 3 SCENE 1

Rehearsal Space/Japanese Tea House
Time: 17:21

1. Rotating Paper Screen
2. Photographic Film
3. Radiator
4. Bookshelf
5. Kitchen
6. Bathroom
7. Performing Platform

Initial ideas › **Development and detail** › **Construction and occupation**

Holly Newnham on the use of a storyboard to connect the ideas behind the project:
I had lost sight of the way that all my preliminary pieces of work together formed my concept. Through creating a storyboard of my process so far, I was able to link all my previous work together to home – in on the things that are important to my design and fill in the gaps where the communication of my process was unclear.

Ralph Saull on the difference between making early conceptual leaps and later considered design choices:
Pigeon steps and somersaults: design ideas feel to me like somersaults, a thrilling jump from A to B. The journey is short, swift and fantastic. Ideas are hard to capture in their fleeting moment. Design choices leave a trail of logic. There is no need to capture them, for the process and method leading to their conception can be observed in reverse. They are self-evident and they tell all. Making design choices can feel like taking tiny pigeon steps in comparison to having an idea, but in their combined outcome the thrill is found.

William Fisher on the use of orthographic drawings to study and resolve a detailed portion of the theatre:
Used the seat and stage models to produce a plan, by taking into account the depth of the stages, the angles they are placed at and how this affects the viewable area in which the audience can sit. Working in section, I then discover the angles required to view over the top of the seats in front. Combining the section and plan allowed me to arrange my seating and provided inspiration for the shape of the theatre.

Technology concepts exercise

During the detail design phase of a project, plastic conceptual ideas must be turned into physical ones. Through the materials that are chosen and the way that they are put together, technology can inspire or express an architectural concept. We all exist in a physical world subject to laws such as gravity and seasonal change. These conditions are influenced by the people who inhabit the world as well as the architects who design for their physical needs. The following exercise seeks to name the links that an architect can make between the concept for their design and its expression through technology. Find a word in the first column that has the most influence on the building or element that you are designing. Find a word in the other columns that relates most closely to the concept of your project. Make a statement explaining how this concept can be expressed through the materials that you select and how you connect them.

Physical conditions influencing architecture	The conceptual qualities of materials and connections	
Gravity	Disguise	Expression
Time	Contrast	Continuity
Climate	Movement	Static
Enclosure	Craft	Technology
Openings	Temporary	Permanent
Culture	Complexity	Simplicity
Resources	Layers	Monolithic
Skill	Mass	Delicacy
	Separation	Connection
	Pristine	Decay
	Quality	Humility
	Tradition	Revolution
	Precision	Randomness
	Human scale	Non-human scale
	Natural	Artificial
	Calm	Restless

Initial ideas › Development and detail › Construction and occupation

**Typical activities
at this stage**

Construction drawings
Design through making
1:1 site samples and
mock-ups
Quality control
Materiality
Research
Decision-making
Control
Feedback
Managing complexity
Collaboration

**Once the architect has produced construction
drawings that are sufficiently detailed to obtain prices
from building contractors and approvals from statutory
bodies, the project can begin on site. Traditionally,
the architect leads the design team of consultants and
channels communication between the contractor and
the client. The architect will manage the project and
control its quality. The architect's production of drawings
and models tends to decrease in proportion to the
completion of the building.**

However, design does not stop at this point. Unexpected
contingencies arise that must be catered for. For example,
a shortage of one material may lead to a redesign of an
element using another material. During construction there
is a gap between the speculation of the drawings and the
reality of the building. This is very similar to the gap between
the idea and the drawing during the initial ideas phase. For
example, standing on the upper levels of the scaffold around
a new building could afford an unanticipated view of a river
and a window may be repositioned to take advantage of it.

During this stage of a project the architect needs to be
aware of the beginnings and the core ideas of the project to
ensure its integrity. Early drawings anticipated the occupation
of the building; the architect will have grown very familiar
with the place and its people by this stage and should remain
sensitive to their reactions to the emerging building. This
important feedback can inform design decisions during
construction. Once the contractor hands back the building
on completion, ownership reverts to the client. The architect
can no longer wander freely within 'their' building or make
any changes to it beyond the correction of mistakes. They
will normally return with the contractor six months or a year
later to agree the remedy of any defects. The occupation
of the building is the first opportunity for the architect's
predictions and innovations to be tested as a whole.

Project: Dovecote Studio
Location: Aldeburgh, Suffolk, UK
Architect: Haworth Tompkins
Date: 2009

This welded COR-TEN steel studio
building was pre-fabricated and
craned into the brick remnants
of a former dovecote to provide
a small studio for musicians, artists
and writers.

Development and detail › **Construction and occupation**

Haworth Tompkins

Haworth Tompkins is an architectural practice based
in London and established by Graham Haworth and Steve
Tompkins. The practice has designed buildings for the public,
private and subsidised sectors, including schools, galleries,
theatres, housing, offices, shops and factories. Both directors
give lectures on their work and Steve Tompkins teaches at
the University of Greenwich, London.

The practice is particularly well known for its innovative arts
projects. The productive nature of these visual, dramatic and
musical arts organisations has inspired Haworth Tompkins
to develop a design strategy of 'provisional' and robust
architecture that suits the creative activities and life of these
places. This thinking was further developed with several
temporary buildings, such as the Almeida Theatre in Kings
Cross, where an economic rough-and-readiness and the
stage-set quality of some elements (lent by the client's
backstage crew fit-out), were both necessary and relished
by architects, client and theatre-goers alike.

Several projects to adapt existing buildings, such as the
Young Vic Theatre in London, have given Haworth Tompkins
the opportunity to consider innovative construction methods,
conceptual possibilities and the tactile effect of materials.

Theatre buildings that spring to life for every performance
heighten the architects' sense that the building is only
really complete when it is occupied. As a result, Haworth
Tompkins' design process is focused on the possibilities
inherent in the life of the building after construction rather
than as an idealised and empty architectural shell.

**Project: Young Vic Theatre
redevelopment
Location: London, UK
Architect: Haworth Tompkins
Date: 2006**

Photograph of the theatre in its
distinctive urban context.

Development and detail › **Construction and occupation**

'On the Young Vic Theatre we spent a lot of time just sitting in performances and sitting in bars in the neighbourhood watching the world go by and understanding what the political and social microclimate was like.'

Steve Tompkins, Haworth Tompkins

Project: Young Vic Theatre redevelopment
Location: London, UK
Architect: Haworth Tompkins
Date: 2006

Illuminated model. As a theatre, the building comes to life at night so the architects have illuminated their model in order to understand the effect that the building will have after dark.

Project: Young Vic Theatre redevelopment
Location: London, UK
Architect: Haworth Tompkins
Date: 2006

Foyer viewed from the retained butcher's shop. The original Young Vic Theatre was built around the shop, the sole survivor on the site of a WWII bomb. The original tiling has been retained and openings formed in a robust, unsentimental way.

Development and detail : **Construction and occupation**

Interview with Haworth Tompkins

What methods do you use to predict the experience of using a building that you are designing?

Graham Haworth

We work with models a lot: three-dimensional massing models, and we always make a site context model very early on. We tend to zoom in and zoom out of scales so we'll be at 1:1250 looking at the infrastructure and the context, and zoom right into 1:5 or 1:20 to look at key spaces.

Steve Tompkins

Often we'll describe the building. We'll begin to describe its personalities and its qualities before we've drawn it. What if you were to walk in and there would be a sense of connection to this part of the brief? We begin to walk through the building before it is a building. In a way you're reversing the normal process of description and presentation.

Project: Snape Maltings
Location: Aldeburgh, UK
Architect: Haworth Tompkins
Date: 2009

Lath ceiling inspired by the materials of the existing buildings at Snape.

Graham Haworth

We don't retreat to the studio to try and work within a boundary of things that are abstract and certain. We like the accidental; we like the slightly edgy, the slightly dangerous things that come out.

Steve Tompkins

By keeping the process aerodynamically unstable for longer than normal you get more interesting results. If you're brave enough and exploratory enough then you acquire a certain authority for that sort of working method. We work best when we have really strong relationships with clients; not just professional relationships, but building up trust and vulnerability so you can actually explore those things. You can think the unthinkable and say the unsayable and it's much more akin to fine art practice in that respect.

Do the parallels between art practice and the craft of building construction help to reinforce the element of craft in your architecture?

Steve Tompkins

I think it very much does that. A lot of the buildings we do end up being hand-finished in one form or another, either by the contractor but often by the client's own teams. We are working with clients who have got production capacity and will often try and build in a phase where we can complete and tune the building with the clients. So decoration, final second fix, fit-out, furniture design – all of those things we've quite often done with direct labour.

How have your collaborations with artists informed your thinking?

Graham Haworth

We often work with artists to amplify the objectives or character of a project. We worked with Jake Tilsen on the London Library and he did a photographic journal of the existing fabric of the building: it's like a palimpsest that's been written over and we wanted that to be made clear. One thing that's interesting working with artists is there's a kind of tension, because of the way we work. You can't just go to your studio and do the perfect pure thing, you're having to engage with the junk of everyday living; people messing with your ideas. Artists are really precise about their work, they don't compromise; they record everything. We do hundreds of sketches; they'll all get thrown away. Artists are very precise about the way things are conceived and working with artists has made us take the conceptual side of our work more seriously.

Steve Tompkins

It's also given us a more dense understanding of material and surface and meaning of material and surface. An artist will spend an enormous amount of time on tactile or pigment quality of the surface and it's made us see those things in a much more detailed way. For example, we've hand-finished a lot of concrete work at Snape because we couldn't specify what we wanted to do, so we ended up doing it ourselves in the way that an artist would do it.

Graham Haworth

There's a poetry in the way that we use materials. It's trying to pick up on poetic and creative themes. So what might be appropriate in Snape, using lath and sandblasted brick with resonances of the shingle beaches, is a poetic response to that landscape.

For a different brief and context we would adopt a different approach; so a building in central London, like the Painting School we're doing for the Royal College of Art, is a factory, basically. There's very little poetry in the use of materials here, which are minimal and industrial. It's very direct and it's going to get kicked about and it's a totally different brief. It would be highly inappropriate to be overtly precious in that space but there is a sensibility about how it goes together. We kept the outside of the building there, because we thought the memory of what it used to be as a factory was important, so we kept the old brick and simply inserted a new steel object inside. At Snape there was much more stuff to work with that's about the history of the place. It's about being appropriate and making the appropriate response. We have a working method that can accommodate a wide range and a wide swing of approaches.

Steve Tompkins

Both Snape Maltings and the Royal College of Art are buildings where creative processes will be happening so the building actually can't tell the whole story. If it did it would choke off the main purpose, which is to have a creative relationship with the space that you're working with. A lot of our projects are about that. They're about knowing where to stop, so that the architecture doesn't dominate or subjugate.

Graham Haworth

They're incomplete in that sense. They're not complete until they are used.

Steve Tompkins

Psychologically, creative people tend to engage more with the space that feels more provisional, more available, more permissive to what they're doing.

Development and detail › Construction and occupation

What can be gained by not tying a design up too tightly?

Steve Tompkins

Often things will happen on site that were unintended, which, because of the methodology and the construction, we were able to commandeer into the finished language of the building; that sort of forgiving aesthetic. It not only means that the finished building is interesting and perhaps more humane but also that it can carry on moving, albeit in slow motion, throughout its life. They are able to accrete change in a way that doesn't feel threatening.

Graham Haworth

The areas we do leave open to change are really carefully controlled. For the Young Vic the contract was to finish the building to within about 95 per cent of the completion in conventional terms and then for the contract to stop, which would mean that the theatre production team could move in, having fitted out the carpentry workshop. We knew that we had the technical capabilities on site within the client body to make that perfectly possible and as a deliberate by-product of that, it meant that the building was owned and absorbed into the creative organisation and they weren't frightened of changes. So you almost gave them permission to take the building on and kick it around, because that's what it's for.

Do you use sample panels to help make decisions about materiality before work starts on site?

Graham Haworth

You need to know what you're getting before you get on site, so the Young Vic panels for example [hand-painted by artist-collaborator Clem Crosby] were mocked up in the studio at first. Most of our projects have a warehouse somewhere with big things in them six months before they're needed. There's one at the moment for the London Library, which has got the Art Room steelwork in it. We've been fiddling with that for the past six months. So one-to-one mock-ups are really essential to us.

Project: Snape Maltings
Location: Aldeburgh, UK
Architect: Haworth Tompkins
Date: 2009

above right:
Foyer to performance spaces. The architects' choice of materials makes the difference between original fabric and new insertions very legible.

below right:
Britten Hall. Acoustic testing in the new hall following construction.

The design project

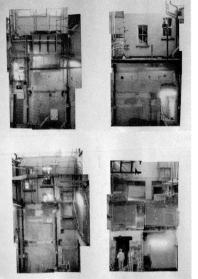

Project: The London Library
Location: St James's Square, London, UK
Architect: Haworth Tompkins
Date: 2010

above:
During the construction phase of the London Library project an existing courtyard lightwell was exposed. Construction work enabled better access to this part of the building than had been possible beforehand, due to the tightness of the site. Provision had been made before renovation began, to assess its qualities during construction. A detailed photographic survey was pinned up in the office to enable discussion on how the space should be treated prior to implementing final design decisions on site.

right:
Architects' drawing of the WC plan detail showing floor tiles by artist Martin Creed, who collaborated with Haworth Tompkins on the project.

The design project

Steve Tompkins

Once you've built a few buildings you realise that a CAD line with a 1.5mm tolerance is a joke and you'd just be exposed as an idiot to go on site and insist on those kinds of tolerances. You've just got to understand the material you're dealing with and make the detailing appropriate to that. The job we've just done in Oxford, the North Wall [Arts Centre] was clad in green oak in shakes and strips. We knew that those strips would move so we detailed it to expect it to twist and move, and for the roof cladding to curl and move around. If you're expecting that not to happen it's a disaster, but if the details welcome it and anticipate it then it's really joyful; that's a part of the texture of the architecture.

What is the best way to understand the way different materials are put together?

Steve Tompkins

One-to-one drawing: a big sheet of paper on the wall, because in CAD it's scaleless and so you actually never necessarily get a sense of seeing the tactile scale of what it is you are designing. So we cover the walls of these rooms with one-to-one details and we sit and sweat over them for an afternoon.

Graham Haworth

At the beginning of the work on site we make a presentation to the builder and talk to him about the design. So often you find that they just get the drawings and they build it and they don't really know why the drawings are the way they are.

Steve Tompkins

In the end, we have to be creative leaders on the project and we have to acquire a strong voice that inspires confidence in everybody else. You can't duck that as an architect so you have to claim the authorship of it, but along the way you can enlist other voices and be self-confident enough to listen as well as lead. It's brilliant when the job is maybe a month from completion and, if you're lucky, you're just getting the sense that it's maybe going to work out and there's that real palpable sense of excitement that somebody has taken your idea seriously enough to build it. It's always a brilliant surprise that never goes away. A childish delight, really.

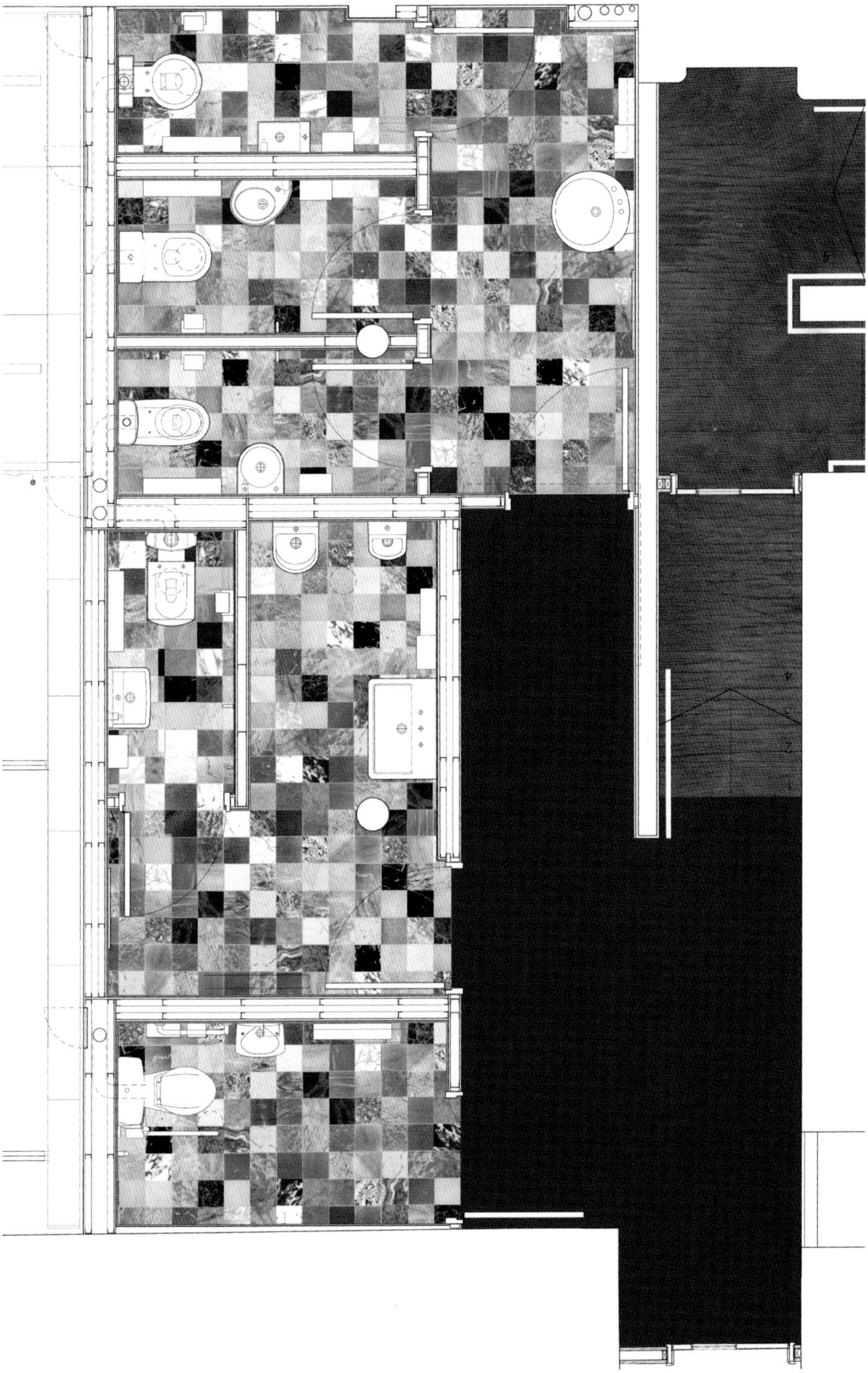

Interview summary

For Haworth Tompkins, consideration of the occupied life of their buildings is integral to their design process, so much so that they consider the building to be incomplete until it is used: both occupied and a little worn at the edges. The design of buildings that are able to cope with change, both daily and over the lifetime of the building, fits particularly well with many of their clients, who are in the business of art production: visual, theatrical and musical. Dialogue with the client is carefully developed from the outset to improve the architects' understanding of the way that the building must be designed to fit the way that it will be occupied.

Haworth Tompkins' work demonstrates a deep understanding of the effect of materials and how they are put together, but also a playfulness in the way that they are used.

Collaboration is key: Haworth Tompkins explore parallels between the craft of the architect and that of the contractor and the artist-collaborators; and also between the production of the client, the artist-collaborators and the contractor. Where skills are shared, opportunities are taken to blur the boundaries between their roles. The architect, the client and artist-collaborators are given opportunities to contribute to the building, making informed and intelligent connections between design, construction and occupation.

Project: The London Library
Location: London, UK
Architect: Haworth Tompkins
Date: 2010

Sectional perspective. Haworth Tompkins populated their drawings for the project with literary figures such as Agatha Christie; Truman Capote; Alfred, Lord Tennyson and Charles Dickens.

'Why do they want to commission a building and work with us? When you start looking at that, you're seeing what your value is, that they are interested in doing something that changes the way they use a building, the way their organisation works, the way they think and experience their day to day.'
Graham Haworth, Haworth Tompkins

Development and detail › Construction and occupation

Cross section

Unfolding *Hamlet* by Joseph Brown. This cross-section drawing of an actor's house designed to unfold and open out into a stage set shows the building occupied by the actor and his party guests.

Sectional perspective

Outdoor theatre for *Romeo and Juliet* by Rodolfo Acevedo Rodriguez. Experiential sectional perspective of cinema, showing occupation and mirrored reflections.

The student experience

This section follows the progress of a group of architecture students as they reach the end of a 12-week design studio project to design an outdoor theatre. The theatre company then commissioned the students to design and build an information booth as a live project.

At the final review students presented process work, orthographic drawings in two and three dimensions and detailed models of their resolved proposals. The drawings represented the function, activity, experience and occupation of each proposal as well as the human and urban scale of the building in context. Models, mock-ups and prototypes were used to explore tangible qualities such as materials and structure. Although the theatre designs were not expected to be built, events such as the final review, portfolio review and end-of-year exhibition brought the opportunity for students to receive feedback on their designs from a wider audience and to test how well their drawings and models communicated to others.

Construction

With the commission to design and build an information booth for the theatre company, the whole design process began again, from client brief and site visit to initial ideas and design development. This time the students were designing as a group, using ideas workshops to generate and test multiple design ideas before agreeing on the ones to develop. The brief was for a demountable, lightweight booth in which to display and hand out information and to sell tickets. Budget, time and construction skills were very real issues that informed the design. A full-scale prototype was constructed to test the design and this improved understanding of material tolerances and buildability. Seeing and trying out the prototype allowed the client and designers to raise issues of ergonomics, usability and materials.

The design project

:20 Accommodation Section
[Fully Exposed]

GLASS

LIGHT CHAMB

Occupation

The revised design was constructed and handed over to the members of the theatre company at a meeting to show them how to mount and demount the booth. The last test was its use in a busy city street where it succeeded in robustly providing visible publicity without obstructing everyday activity.

Ralph Saull anticipating the effects of change and the passage of time in his design studio project:
Why do we programme change and flexibility into our architecture? Is it so the sense of possibility is preserved? My design will not just allow for change and decay, but depend on it. The materials I specify will mature to define the aesthetic of the complete; not decay and break the sense of completion.

Rodolfo Acevedo Rodriguez on why it is necessary to design with the intended occupation of the building in mind:
Building, machine and body come together. The materiality and function are the product of an interaction between them; how one thing relates to another is defined by dimension and detail, but how the space will become inhabitable depends simply on how well all elements are compared and layered.

Anna Beer (Information Booth live project) on the continuation of design activity into the construction phase:
Initially, we had thought of using a lightweight construction fabric with a rod support skeleton, to contrast with the more solid frame of the actual booth; however, this caused problems because we couldn't find a way of supporting a lightweight fabric in the preferred concertina shape without adding significantly to the stress on the ticket booth. We solved this by adding a back wall to the ticket booth which attached to the roof in an upside-down L-shape. Even with a 'final design', the ticket booth was constantly morphing and we were constantly questioning it. The construction was definitely a learning curve.

Prototype design exercise

As the project progresses, the architect is required to design at every scale and level of detail. The most critical decisions are made first and are followed by secondary decisions. There is no one right way to prioritise this: an architectural concept can begin with the design of a light fitting and end with the roof or vice versa. It depends on the requirements of each project and the sensibility of the architect. Studio-based projects place less emphasis on the construction phase, but it is possible to explore this aspect of architecture in the studio, such as the example below, to help develop a design project and design skills.

1 Design a prototype element to be found within the proposed project. This could be a door handle, a piece of furniture, a window or even a new material.

2 Make the element or part-element, preferably using the actual materials proposed.

This process acts as a testing ground for the application of conceptual ideas. It enables you to gain invaluable feedback on your proposals while still in the process of designing the overall project. It also provides material and textural information that can be fed back into smaller-scale representations of the project. If there is enough scope within the project, the process can be taken further:

3 Make an instruction booklet describing how to make the piece. Communicate with a level of graphic quality and detail that would enable a third party to make the piece without further instruction.

This provides valuable experience in preparing drawings that can be read by a contractor and will also enable you to think through the process from inception to completion.

The interviews with the five architectural practices in Chapter 3 reveal some of the values and approaches that they share. They all have ambitions for their projects that go beyond the apparent scope of the initial brief and they look beyond their own immediate discipline into areas as diverse as art practice, politics, craft, music, material science, philosophy, literature and theatre.

Collaborative ways of working with people both inside and outside the construction industry and the use of working methods from other disciplines nourish the work of each architect. An interest in the human condition also underpinned much of the discussion. Each architect spoke with great skill to communicate complex ideas. Articulating ideas in an engaging way is not only important for communication with clients, contractors and other interested parties, it also allows the architect to test and search for meaning in discussion with their colleagues. Instinctive moves were analysed and understood by the architects. Threads linking their own work were picked up and sense made of them. Patterns were established and interrogated.

Where the architects differed in their attitudes and approaches, issues of emphasis, specialisation and agenda were present. The will to innovate and to pursue a line of enquiry has led each of the five practices to develop different areas of expertise such as participatory methods, trans-disciplinary explorations and material innovations. The precise nature of this emphasis varies, but each new project forms the next step in the overall development of a practice's pursuit of meaning in their work. Graphical communication must respond to these variations in approach and the architect must use all of their skills to represent the qualities of their design and do it justice.

The aim of this book is to act as a guide to design-studio culture, enabling everyone to participate fully on their own terms; to give you knowledge and therefore control over your own design process; and to offer inspiration with examples of the work and working methods of different architects. Where possible, mysteries surrounding the learning and activities of architectural design have been unravelled or, at the very least, the reasons for their existence explained.

Project: From Earth Literary Festival
Location: Oxford, UK
Designer: Huda Jaber
Date: 2010

Architectural design

One of the greatest difficulties in writing a book about
architectural design is that it is essentially a practical, active
application of ideas. Reading this book in isolation, without
also being immersed in the activity of designing, would be
like learning to play the piano by correspondence course and
without an instrument. The interviews, illustrated examples
of work and the techniques sections will allow you to 'learn
by example' and 'learn by doing' as you would in the design
studio. Read the book in a creative, non-linear way and
plunder it for whatever information you need for your projects.

Bibliography

The design studio

January 2006. Architects' Offices
Architecture and Urbanism, 424

Hart V, 2002. Nicholas Hawksmoor
Rebuilding Ancient Wonders
New Haven and London: Yale University
Press for the Paul Mellon Centre for Studies
in British Art

Priest, C & Anderson, J, 2009
*OB1 Year One Architecture and Interior
Architecture*, Oxford Brookes University
[online], available at:
http://ob1architecture.blogspot.com

Stevens, G, 2009
*A History of Architectural Education in the
West* [online], available at:
http://www.archsoc.com/kcas/Historyed.html

Whitford, F, 1984
Bauhaus
London: Thames and Hudson Ltd

The design process

Elkins, J, 2001
*Why Art Cannot Be Taught:
a Handbook for Art Students.*
Urbana and Chicago: University of
Illinois Press

Frederick, M, 2007
101 Things I Learned in Architecture School
Cambridge, Massachusetts and London:
The MIT Press

Gänshirt, C, 2007
*Tools for Ideas: Introduction to Architectural
Design*
Basel: Birkhäuser Verlag AG

Architectural design

Atelier Bow-Wow, 2007
Graphic Anatomy
Tokyo: Toto

CHORA, Bunschoten, R, Hoshino, T
& Binet H, 2001
Urban Flotsam. Stirring the City
Rotterdam: 010 Publishers

Jessen, D, Lewis, J & Lösing, J, 2009
Expressing Interest
East

Littlefield, D & Lewis, S, 2007
*Architectural Voices: Listening to Old
Buildings*
Chichester: Wiley

O'Donnell, S & Tuomey, J, 2007
O'Donnell + Tuomey
New York: Princeton Architectural Press

Snøhetta, 2007
*Conditions. Snøhetta. Architecture. Interior.
Landscape*
Baden: Lars Müller Publishers

Snøhetta, 2009
*Snøhetta Works. Architecture. Interior.
Landscape*
Baden: Lars Müller Publishers

Tuomey, J, 2004
Architecture, Craft and Culture
Oysterhaven: Gandon Editions

Architects

AOC
Second Floor
101 Redchurch Street
London E2 7DL
UK
+44 020 7739 9950
www.theaoc.co.uk

Atelier Bow Wow
8–79 Suga-cho Shinjuku-ku
Tokyo
Japan 160–0018
+81 03 3226 5336
www.bow-wow.jp

CHORA architecture and urbanism
24a Bartholomew Villas
London NW5 2LL
UK
+44 020 7267 1277
www.chora.org

East
4th floor, 49–59 Old Street
London EC1V 9HX
UK
+44 020 7490 3190
www.east.uk.com

Haworth Tompkins
19 – 20 Great Sutton Street
London EC1V 0DR
UK
+44 020 7250 3225
www.haworthtompkins.com

Klein Dytham architecture
AD Bldg 2F
1-15-7 Hiroo
Shibuya-ku
Tokyo 150-0012
Japan
www.klein-dytham.com

NL Architects
Van Hallstraat 294
NL 1051 HM
Amsterdam
+31 020 620 73 23
www.nlarchitects.nl

O'Donnell + Tuomey Architects
20A Camden Row
Dublin 8
Ireland
+353 1 475 2500
www.odonnell-tuomey.ie

SHoP Architects PC
11 Park Place Penthouse
New York
NY 10007
USA
+1 212 889 9005
www.shoparc.com

Snøhetta AS
Skur 39, Vippetangen
N-0150 Oslo
Norway
+47 24 15 60 60
www.snoarc.no

Zaha Hadid
10 Bowling Green Lane
London EC1R 0BQ
UK
+44 020 7253 5147
www.zaha-hadid.com

Architectural design

Compiled by Indexing Specialists (UK) Ltd, Indexing House, 306A Portland Road, Hove, East Sussex BN3 5LP. Tel: 01273 416777. Email: indexers@indexing.co.uk Website: www.indexing.co.uk

Page numbers in italics refer to illustrations.

A special debt of gratitude is owed to the architectural practices who generously gave their time to talk to me and contribute images for publication. Their willingness to talk about their work with such insight and openness was critical to the development of the book. I would like to thank: Julian Lewis, Dann Jessen and Judith Lösing of East; Raoul Bunschoten of CHORA; John Tuomey and Sheila O'Donnell of O'Donnell + Tuomey Architects; Craig Dykers and Kjetil Thorsen of Snøhetta; and Graham Haworth and Steve Tompkins of Haworth Tompkins.

Thanks are also due to those who kindly contributed images of their work and information about it and also those who helped with the sourcing of images and the setting up of the interviews: Kamiel Klaasse of NL Architects; Tiffany A Taraska of SHoP Architects; Dirk Lellau and Liva Dudareva of CHORA; Monika Hinz of O'Donnell + Tuomey Architects; Elin Nilsen and Karianne Pedersen of Snøhetta; Brian Yeats of Haworth Tompkins; Emi Takahashi of Klein Dytham architecture; Davide Giordano of Zaha Hadid Architects; Christian Gänshirt; Kate Goodwin and Simone Sagi of the Royal Academy; Joseph Grima of Storefront for Art and Architecture; Wells Cathedral Stonemasons and Nigel Hiscock.

Thank you to Rachel Netherwood, Caroline Walmsley and Leafy Robinson at AVA Publishing and Jane Harper for the design of the book.

In particular I would like to thank Helena Webster for first suggesting that I write this book, Professor Mark Swenarton, John Stevenson, Colin Priest, Emmanuel Dupont and Carsten Jungfer of the Department of Architecture, Oxford Brookes University and my former colleague, Ana Araujo.

A special acknowledgement is due to the student contributors of images and design diary entries: Rodolfo Acevedo Rodriguez, Anna Beer, Joseph Brown, Elliott Cohen, Ryan Doran, Edmund Drury, William Fisher, Gavin Fraser, Joanna Gorringe Minto, Geoffrey Howells, Huda Jaber, John Marshall, Heena Mistry, Jack Morton-Gransmore, Jonathan Motzafi-Haller, Holly Newnham, Ralph Saull, U Ieong To, Justus Van Der Hoven, Esther Vince, James Williamson, Farah Yusof and Anna Zezula. And of course, thank you First Year, whose energy and originality inspired this book.

This book could not have happened without the support of my family. Thank you.

BASICS
ARCHITECTURE

Working with ethics

Lynne Elvins
Naomi Goulder

Publisher's note

The subject of ethics is not new, yet its consideration within the applied visual arts is perhaps not as prevalent as it might be. Our aim here is to help a new generation of students, educators and practitioners find a methodology for structuring their thoughts and reflections in this vital area.

AVA Publishing hopes that these **Working with ethics** pages provide a platform for consideration and a flexible method for incorporating ethical concerns in the work of educators, students and professionals. Our approach consists of four parts:

The **introduction** is intended to be an accessible snapshot of the ethical landscape, both in terms of historical development and current dominant themes.

The **framework** positions ethical consideration into four areas and poses questions about the practical implications that might occur. Marking your response to each of these questions on the scale shown will allow your reactions to be further explored by comparison.

The **case study** sets out a real project and then poses some ethical questions for further consideration. This is a focus point for a debate rather than a critical analysis so there are no predetermined right or wrong answers.

A selection of **further reading** for you to consider areas of particular interest in more detail.

ethical: awareness/ reflection/ debate

Working with ethics

Ethics is a complex subject that interlaces the idea of responsibilities to society with a wide range of considerations relevant to the character and happiness of the individual. It concerns virtues of compassion, loyalty and strength, but also of confidence, imagination, humour and optimism. As introduced in ancient Greek philosophy, the fundamental ethical question is: *what should I do?* How we might pursue a 'good' life not only raises moral concerns about the effects of our actions on others, but also personal concerns about our own integrity.

In modern times the most important and controversial questions in ethics have been the moral ones. With growing populations and improvements in mobility and communications, it is not surprising that considerations about how to structure our lives together on the planet should come to the forefront. For visual artists and communicators, it should be no surprise that these considerations will enter into the creative process.

Some ethical considerations are already enshrined in government laws and regulations or in professional codes of conduct. For example, plagiarism and breaches of confidentiality can be punishable offences. Legislation in various nations makes it unlawful to exclude people with disabilities from accessing information or spaces. The trade of ivory as a material has been banned in many countries. In these cases, a clear line has been drawn under what is unacceptable.

But most ethical matters remain open to debate, among experts and lay-people alike, and in the end we have to make our own choices on the basis of our own guiding principles or values. Is it more ethical to work for a charity than for a commercial company? Is it unethical to create something that others find ugly or offensive?

Specific questions such as these may lead to other questions that are more abstract. For example, is it only effects on humans (and what they care about) that are important, or might effects on the natural world require attention too?

Is promoting ethical consequences justified even when it requires ethical sacrifices along the way? Must there be a single unifying theory of ethics (such as the Utilitarian thesis that the right course of action is always the one that leads to the greatest happiness of the greatest number), or might there always be many different ethical values that pull a person in various directions?

As we enter into ethical debate and engage with these dilemmas on a personal and professional level, we may change our views or change our view of others. The real test though is whether, as we reflect on these matters, we change the way we act as well as the way we think. Socrates, the 'father' of philosophy, proposed that people will naturally do 'good' if they know what is right. But this point might only lead us to yet another question: *how do we know what is right?*

You
What are your ethical beliefs?

Central to everything you do will be your attitude to people and issues around you. For some people, their ethics are an active part of the decisions they make every day as a consumer, a voter or a working professional. Others may think about ethics very little and yet this does not automatically make them unethical. Personal beliefs, lifestyle, politics, nationality, religion, gender, class or education can all influence your ethical viewpoint.

Using the scale, where would you place yourself? What do you take into account to make your decision? Compare results with your friends or colleagues.

Your client
What are your terms?

Working relationships are central to whether ethics can be embedded into a project, and your conduct on a day-to-day basis is a demonstration of your professional ethics. The decision with the biggest impact is whom you choose to work with in the first place. Cigarette companies or arms traders are often-cited examples when talking about where a line might be drawn, but rarely are real situations so extreme. At what point might you turn down a project on ethical grounds and how much does the reality of having to earn a living affect your ability to choose?

Using the scale, where would you place a project? How does this compare to your personal ethical level?

01 02 03 04 05 06 07 08 09 10

01 02 03 04 05 06 07 08 09 10

Your specifications
What are the impacts of your materials?

In relatively recent times, we are learning that many natural materials are in short supply. At the same time, we are increasingly aware that some man-made materials can have harmful, long-term effects on people or the planet. How much do you know about the materials that you use? Do you know where they come from, how far they travel and under what conditions they are obtained? When your creation is no longer needed, will it be easy and safe to recycle? Will it disappear without a trace? Are these considerations your responsibility or are they out of your hands?

Using the scale, mark how ethical your material choices are.

Your creation
What is the purpose of your work?

Between you, your colleagues and an agreed brief, what will your creation achieve? What purpose will it have in society and will it make a positive contribution? Should your work result in more than commercial success or industry awards? Might your creation help save lives, educate, protect or inspire? Form and function are two established aspects of judging a creation, but there is little consensus on the obligations of visual artists and communicators toward society, or the role they might have in solving social or environmental problems. If you want recognition for being the creator, how responsible are you for what you create and where might that responsibility end?

Using the scale, mark how ethical the purpose of your work is.

01 02 03 04 05 06 07 08 09 10

01 02 03 04 05 06 07 08 09 10

Working with ethics

One aspect of architecture that raises an ethical dilemma is that of sheer scale and therefore the environmental impact of the materials and energy required to create and use buildings. Construction of buildings and their use account for around half of all greenhouse gas emissions and energy consumed in the US each year. Waste from the construction industry in the UK is three times that of waste from all domestic use and many building materials are considered hazardous and require specialist waste treatments.

As the people who create the early stage designs for buildings before construction takes place, architects are well placed to realise buildings that operate with less energy and use less materials. This can be accomplished through a great number of approaches; from proper siting, material selection or day-lighting strategies. But how much responsibility should an architect have for the impacts of buildings when they work alongside town planners, housing developers or building regulators? Is it up to these people to request and plan for more sustainable architecture or should architects have the influence and inclination to change to the way we live?

The mid-nineteenth century saw the rise in state-supported treatment of the mentally ill in the US and consequently, there was a rise in the building of public 'lunatic asylums'. Dr Thomas Story Kirkbride was a founding member of the Association of Medical Superintendents of American Institutions for the Insane (AMSAII). He promoted a standardised method of asylum construction and mental health treatment, known as the 'Kirkbride Plan'. The first asylum opened in New Jersey in 1847.

The building itself was meant to have a curative effect and was considered 'a special apparatus for the care of lunacy'. Each building followed the same basic floor plan described as a 'shallow V', where central administration buildings were flanked by two wings of tiered wards. Wards were to be short enough that a breeze of fresh air could be carried through them and have spacious windows to let in light. Wards for the most difficult patients had single corridors, which made surveillance easier and security better. At a time when few private homes had central heating, gas or toilets, Kirkbride Buildings incorporated gas lamps in each room, central water tanks above the administration centre, and boilers in the basements that heated air to be pumped into wards.